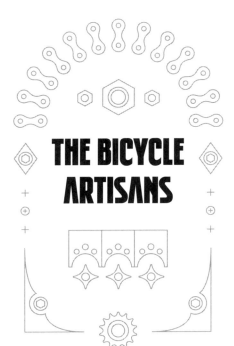

THE BICYCLE
ARTISANS

THE BICYCLE ARTISANS

Will Jones

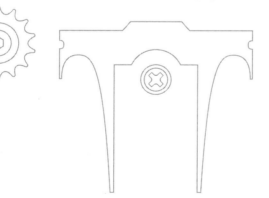

with 617 illustrations, 577 in colour

 Thames & Hudson

CONTENTS

TRANSPORT THAT TRANSCENDS TIME AND TECHNOLOGY

The bicycle makes no sense today. Why attempt to manually propel yourself using pedal power when there are so many different types of mechanized transport? Come to think of it, why travel at all when you can link with anyone, anywhere in the world, in an instant via digital media and virtual face-time? The bicycle would seem to be a relic of a bygone era in the history of transportation. Its method of propulsion is outmoded, its speed outstripped, even the material that most bikes are made of – steel – is a product of yesteryear. The bicycle is dead, or is it?

There are certain parts of the globe that are not as advanced, less affluent, and in these places the bicycle is still a vital mode of transport, used to carry people and cargo because it is cheap to buy, easy to maintain and free to fuel. The reasons are the same that once popularized the bicycle in the developed world, but now there are other options. Countries such as China and India are now rapidly catching up – or rather, leading the way – with new technologies, so the argument that the bicycle is still alive and kicking because of its use there is null and void, because soon everyone will have a car, despite what the pop song says. The bicycle is dead, or is it?

ALIVE AND PEDALLING

Even in the richest countries of the world, cycling is growing in popularity. What is making us technologically savvy folk look to this super-simple, centuries-old mode of transport? Ask any cyclist, and he or she will list a wide range of reasons, from lessening one's environmental impact to navigating quickly through traffic-clogged cities, being able to lug things from one place to the next without the need for a car to simply experiencing the freedom of freewheeling through the streets. The fact is that there is no one reason why cycling is popular, and there never has been. Bicycles in their many forms were invented as workhorses, recreational vehicles, racing machines – everything from the wooden velocipedes and penny farthings of the mid-nineteenth century to the first pneumatic-tyred bikes, tandems and tricycles, through to the recumbent, randonneur, BMX and mountain bikes of today, were designed and built to ride on and overcome all manner of terrain.

The relentless innovation and variety is why bicycles continue to appeal to riders of all different types, and prompts constant development and diversification in the creation of them. From one-man workshops to larger companies, which use the latest technologies (such as wind tunnels) to produce ever-more aerodynamic machines, to online outfits that enable enthusiasts to build a bike from a pick-and-mix assortment of parts, the choice of where to go for your own custom-designed, made-to-measure bike is endless. In the 1970s bespoke frame-builders tended towards track and stripped-down road bikes, but today artisans have widened their remit to satisfy the demands of their increasingly varied client groups, from the city commuter who wants the perfect bicycle for the daily grind to the eco-enthusiast who yearns for mobility yet needs to transport cargo. Then there are the cyclists who just want to have fun – the mountain bikers, BMX kids, freestyle fixed-wheel trick-pullers, randonneurs, racers and plain old leisure riders. The bicycle, it would appear, is alive and kicking.

This book provides a snapshot of these diverse makers, discovering the ideas and technologies that lie behind their designs. Most importantly, it aims to capture the inspirations and enthusiasm that goes into designing and building bicycles for today's cyclists. The artisans included within these pages build all of the types of bicycle mentioned above – and more. They have been chosen for the bikes that they build and the way in which they build them, but above all for the passion they exude about their chosen profession – a word that seems somehow insufficient when listening to these designers speak about their obsession with their craft and riding.

The results of this passion are the bicycles themselves, some of which will cost just a few hundred pounds, while others will set you back many thousands. Most are still built out of steel, but some are built from titanium, aluminium, carbon-fibre, even boron. The material of choice is dependent upon many variables – twenty-first-century artisans can afford to push boundaries and experiment with new technologies because the bicycle is currently undergoing a renaissance. Cycling is gaining more and more followers as bicycle-makers come up with newer, better models to suit the modern urban rider: high-tech materials elevate the humble pushbike into a new scientific realm, and custom designs

express individual personalities more evocatively than any car could. Cycling is popular because the bicycle is timeless – constantly evolving and yet essentially the same. It has adapted with time, and is still in demand despite the relentless onward march of the car.

Put simply, pedal power rules.

OLD SCHOOL, NEW WAVE

Handmade, bespoke, custom-designed, unique, one of a kind, tailored, made to measure ... There are many ways of describing something that has been produced just for you, and the demand for this individuality remains insatiable. We seem to be continually striving for some new way of personalizing our lives, from the choice of playlist on our smart phone to the toppings on our salad at the takeaway counter to the photos we post on Facebook. Take the bespoke suit – who wouldn't want one if they could afford it? A suit that fits perfectly, from the length of the sleeve to the fit across the chest and width of the leg, and meets every style requirement is universally covetable – plus, it makes you look fantastic. This desire to look good, even at a cost, has been around since mankind began to wear clothes – or at least since we began to pay for them. But a tailor-made bicycle, really?

Those in the know will tell you that the reasons for commissioning a custom-made bike are pretty much the same as when ordering a bespoke suit: first is a perfect fit with regards to comfort, use (in the cyclist's case, type of riding) and style, and running a close second is that it will make you look darn good, too. Road-bike specialist Dave Anderson of Anderson Cycles (pp. 22–3) in St Paul, Minnesota,

explains the appeal: 'A truly handmade bike is designed and built for you, and you alone. It will fit you perfectly, and will be built with materials and components that reflect your riding style. A custom bicycle also allows you to be part of the creative process and to experience the rewards of having something built by hand, especially for you. In other words, with a custom bike, you really can have it all.'

Jason McBain of the Canadian firm Concept Bikes (pp. 76–7) thinks the increased interest in cycling and custom-built bikes is due to nobler concerns, citing 'a worldwide awareness of fitness and a move towards eco-consciousness', a view shared by Lennard Zinn of Zinn Cycles (pp. 278–9), in Boulder, Colorado, who notes that 'the urge to buy local and support small businesses is strong today'. But whether ordering a custom-made bike for superficial or more altruistic reasons, all will acknowledge that part of the allure is also about having a bike that no one else has got.

THE NEW REVOLUTION

The builders themselves take on the challenge of creating the ultimate tailor-made bike for many reasons, but getting rich quick isn't one of them. The hours of painstaking work that go into hand-building a bicycle could never be adequately rewarded by anyone but a deliriously carefree millionaire, and yet custom bike-builders are springing up all over the world – why? The answer is surprisingly simple: these guys love cycling. Almost invariably there will be tales of childhoods spent riding bikes, and teen years spent racing and whiling away hours at school in the metalwork shop. The natural progression for these outdoors-loving, steel-bending folk was to build a bicycle: first their own, then for their friends, and finally for a paying clientele.

But what is it that keeps so many of our artisans in the game of frame-building, long after they realize that they can't make a mint? It is, simply, the drive to perfect their craft, the love of the product they produce and an appreciation of the history behind their profession. But times have been hard. Mass production, new materials, rising costs of steel and global economic crises have all affected the world of the custom bike-builder. Against all odds, there has been a resurgence in the sector, and these old-school craftsmen acknowledge that technological progress is to be credited, sort of. Michael Downes of Art & Industry (pp. 24–9) in Portland, Oregon, says of this new embracing of the hand-crafted: 'It has nothing to do with cycling directly, but rather a general reaction against a mass-produced existence. Custom frame-building follows what has happened to beer, food, crafts, music and many other areas. The digital revolution has put direct knowledge and techniques into the hands of individuals, unfiltered by commerce. We are entering the age of the maker.'

Halfway across the world in Sydney, Australia, Paul Hillbrick of Hillbrick Bicycles (pp. 130–1) agrees: 'I think the mass-production market has commoditized bicycles and taken value away from them. Also, many people who have come into cycling in the last ten years have no appreciation for the classic made-to-measure frame. Those who do get to ride a custom bicycle, however, quickly develop a real respect for the craftsmanship and importance of the hand-built product.'

'Mass consumerism is reaching a threshold of sorts for many parts of Western society,' believes Peter Richardson of London's Wren Bicycles (pp.

272–3), 'and the Internet has massively revolutionized the availability of "stuff" over the past decade. Everything is available, everywhere and all the time. People are looking for something different or special that goes against this trend. They are pushing back against the norm and the over-inflated super-brands in all aspects of consumerism.' James Selman of Beloved Cycles (pp. 40–1), also based in Portland, Oregon, puts it simply: 'Why has there been a resurgence in custom-built bikes? It's the search for true craft and identity.'

At the end of the day, ordering a custom-made bicycle is merely a step up, albeit an expensive one, from choosing the fillings in your sarnie or ordering a decaf skinny Americano with a sprinkling of cinnamon. Admittedly, spending weeks and months working with a custom bike-builder to create the perfect bicycle is a bit more laborious than deciding to go with extra lettuce, olives and mayo on your six-inch meat feast, so why do it? We do it in order to feel special, to reassert a little piece of our individuality into at least part of our everyday lives. We do it to make our mark upon this world of mass production, globalization, unification and assimilation.

Now, I'll have fillet-brazed lugs, forged dropouts and fat 29-inchers with that custom paint job, please. No, I don't want the chain guard and fender combo. And I'll get it to take away.

ACHIELLE

Achielle's byline – 'vintage and nostalgic bicycles' – makes it clear where this Belgian company's priorities lie. Achielle is a family-run business, established in 1946 when Achiel Oosterlinck opened a small bicycle shop in Zwevezele, Belgium, selling models from a number of different manufacturers. Achiel branched out into building bicycle designs of his own with his son Jan, and in 1963 founded Dija, which specialized in making a style of bicycle frames similar to those offered by the company today.

Achiel eventually moved the business to Egem in 1976, where he continued to produce bicycle frames to suit the trends of the day, making material and design advances all the while. Ten years later he founded Oostcolor, a sister company that focused on painted bicycle frames, and the two companies soon joined to become Dija-Oostcolor.

It was not for another twenty years that the team considered designing and building vintage-inspired bicycles, but today the company is firmly established in a highly competitive market as a maker of traditional bicycles featuring lugged frames and crowned forks, as well as individual serial numbers on the carrier plate. Achiel's grandsons Tom and Peter now run the company, alongside Jan. Their mandate is to build bicycles that are every bit as beautiful as the ones their grandfather used to make.

ESTABLISHED:	1946
LOCATION:	Egem, Belgium
BIKE TYPE MADE:	Vintage-inspired urban bicycles
SPECIALITIES:	Vintage-inspired handmade bicycles, built with the innovation of today – 'from tube to bicycle in one company'
FAVOURITE RIDER:	Warre Oosterlinck, Jan's three-year-old grandson – 'riding his bicycle like he is going to win the Tour of Flanders'
FAVOURITE BICYCLE:	'Every bicycle made with a soul, and used with love'
FAVOURITE OBJECT:	The bicycle

ANDERSON CYCLES

On his website, Dave Anderson poses the question 'why Anderson Custom?' and goes on to admit that there are 'a lot of "custom" build-ers out there these days'. His acknowledgment of the competition is somewhat at odds with many other bike builders' homepages, but most will readily own up to the challenge of getting noticed in an ever-more crowded market.

Dave stakes his claim by pointing to his skills. 'I build bikes that I believe are as good or better than any others out there,' he says simply. 'Though phrases that include words like "custom" or "handmade" have become overused and clichéd, I do build truly handmade bicycles, with all of the skill and care that someone buying such a machine should expect. I do it all from start to fin-ish, including the finish. No one touches your bike but me, from the time the tubes are pulled off the shelf until you pull it out of the box on delivery.'

Dave specializes in road bikes and tourers, but will build tan-dems and recumbents if asked. 'What it comes down to is that I love bicycles,' he says, 'and building custom bicycles, no matter what type, is something that I am very passionate about.' Dave is at pains to reiterate that a genuinely handmade bike is designed and built for the client, and only the client: 'A good custom bike will also say a lot about you, your personal tastes and your sense of style. Enough said.'

ESTABLISHED:	1995
LOCATION:	St Paul, Minnesota, USA
BIKE TYPE MADE:	Road, cyclocross and a four-seasons all-rounder
SPECIALITIES:	Custom bicycles, frame sets and stainless steel
FAVOURITE RIDER:	Greg LeMond
FAVOURITE BICYCLE:	Bikes by Richard Sachs
FAVOURITE OBJECT:	The Hoover Dam – 'the sheer size of the project and the times in which it was built have always fascinated me'

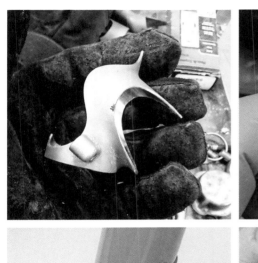

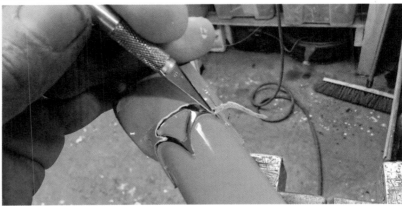

ART & INDUSTRY

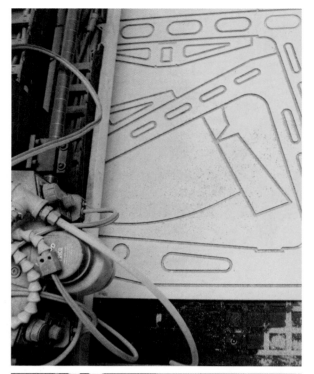

When industrial designer Michael Downes formed Art & Industry as an umbrella company in 2010, under which he could develop concepts that were not part of his day job, it could have been called a hobby, but it is a hobby that has spawned one of the most unique and hard-working bike designs out there. Today, Michael and his team, in collaboration with shipwright Jeff Sayler, design and build wooden cargo bikes. 'I wanted to build a cargo bike and was inspired by the likes of Renovo, which makes wooden frames,' he says. 'Jeff is an experienced boat builder with access to all the equipment I could want, and so it seemed like the perfect fit. That, and the fact that I can't weld or braze for shit!'

Michael has been into cycling since his mid-twenties, when he was a bicycle courier in his native London. An extended stint as a bike mechanic, followed by a period studying industrial design at the Art Center College of Design in Pasadena, California, landed him an internship at Giant in 2000. While at Giant, Michael designed the Simple cruiser, which to his astonishment, Giant put into production. He still rides his Simple today. Wood (plywood, and now bamboo) is his material of choice for the imaginatively titled No. 2 cable-steered cargo bike, the second model in this vein, which wowed the crowds at the Oregon Manifest exhibition. Since then, Michael has continued to push innovations in the utility-bike sector.

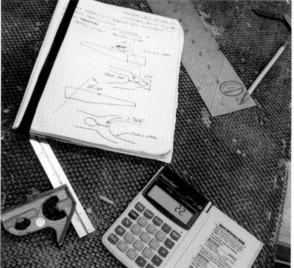

When asked why he believes there has been a resurgence in bespoke bikes, he points out that the custom frame-building revolution is a reflection of the craft movement in other sectors, citing the massive microbrewing trend, in Portland especially, as well as in food and music. 'We are', he says, 'entering the age of the maker.'

ESTABLISHED:	2010
LOCATION:	'People's Republic of Portland', Oregon, USA
BIKE TYPE MADE:	Bakfiets-style cargo bicycle
SPECIALITIES:	'Exploring the intersection between bicycles and boats with particular reference to composite wood structures'
FAVOURITE RIDER:	'That would be me ...'
FAVOURITE BICYCLE:	Dursley Pedersen
FAVOURITE OBJECT:	'That little plastic widget you use to seal the bread bag: simple, reliable, unremarkable – a perfect product'

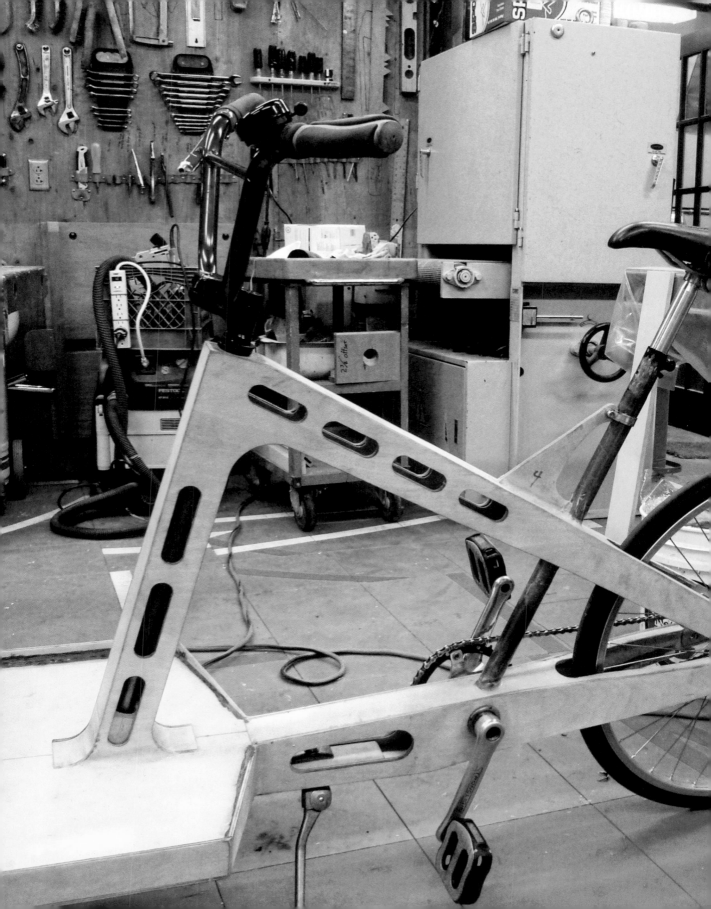

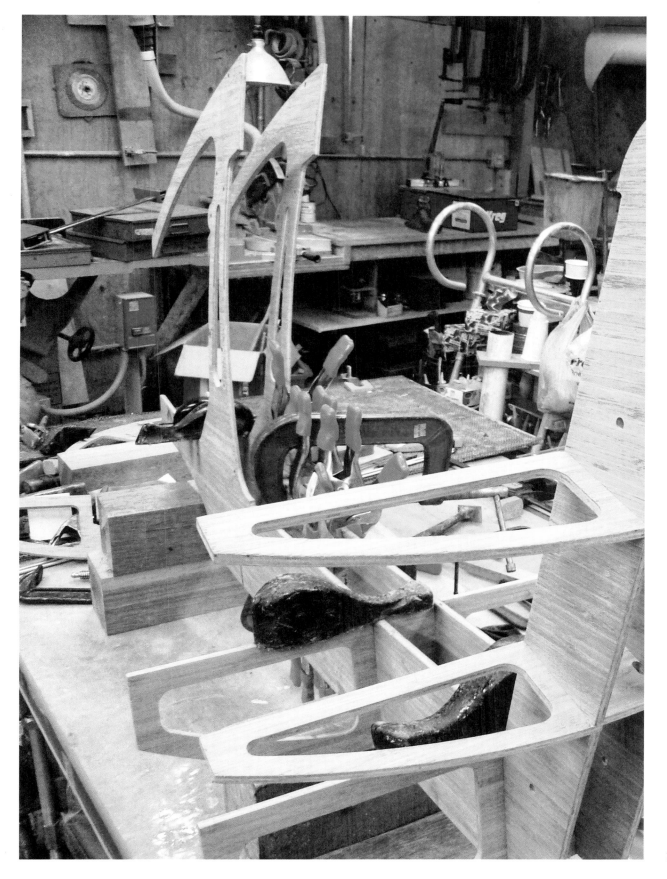

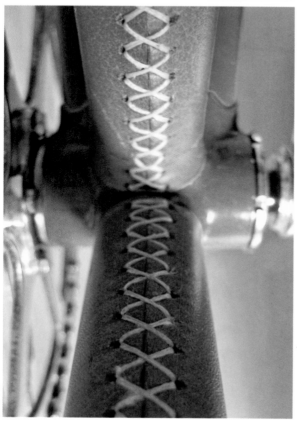

ATELIERS D'EMBELLIE

Nicolas Yvars is not a bicycle designer, he's a marketing man for the sporting-goods industry. But Nicolas also has a trio of passions – leather-craft, vintage fashion and cycling – which he has combined to produce something that truly evokes his love of riding: the Porteur. The first bicycle design to be showcased by his company Ateliers d'Embellie, the Porteur, Nicolas says, 'matches the agility and reactivity of the track frame with an urban ingenuity born of fat tyres and a large front rack.'

But the Porteur is about much more than performance or practicality. Nicolas took months to find the components for his bicycle, sourcing them from vintage suppliers and custom builders. The frame is a French Haral track made from Reynolds 531 tubing, and the fork and headset from a Campagnolo Nuovo Record with C-cup. Nicolas then set about covering the bike with leather, a wrapping inspired by the exquisite craftsmanship of years gone by. 'From the leather to the head badge, I completed most of the work myself,' he says. 'It is all handmade. I did entrust the painting of the frame and wheel mountings to the professionals, though.'

The result is a unique bicycle with such delightful quirks as a stylish, leather-covered drinks flask, tucked under the saddle, and amber-shellacked orange cotton-taped handlebars. The Porteur has attracted a wealth of attention for this French artisan, who is at pains to state that he is not a bicycle designer. It's a shame the bicycle was a one-off, but keep watching Ateliers d'Embellie for more idiosyncratic takes on bicycle design.

ESTABLISHED:	2008
LOCATION:	Grenoble, France
BIKE TYPE MADE:	Vintage bicyclettes, porteurs and city bikes
SPECIALITIES:	Leather-covered bikes and parts
FAVOURITE RIDER:	Mat Hoffman
FAVOURITE BICYCLE:	A. Faure randonneuse (1952)
FAVOURITE OBJECT:	Riva Aquariva Super yacht

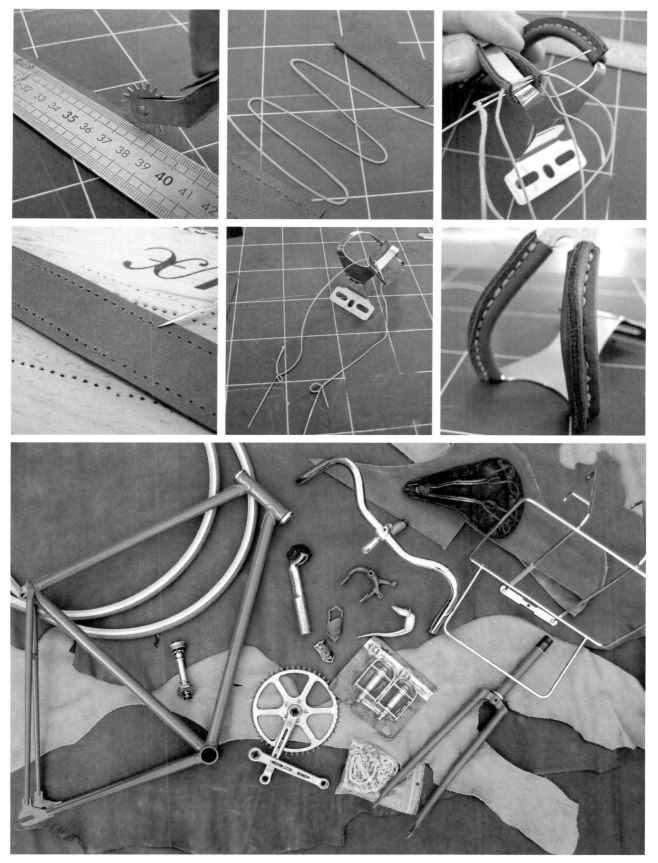

A-TRAIN CYCLES

A relative newcomer to the bike-building world, Alex Cook of A-Train Cycles has been plying his trade for just over five years. His newbie status doesn't show, however, in designs that encompass road, cyclocross, touring, mountain, even fat snow bikes. Alex took up frame-building after working in a bicycle shop and 'living the cycling lifestyle'. His choice of career is a perfect fit, he says, because it's an outlet for his creativity, and because he is and always has been passionate about cycling.

Alex will take on most projects, but prefers it when they present a challenge. As he puts it, 'I especially like the odd and unique, including fat bikes, offset racks, and anything else that might involve a bit of head-scratching and napkin-doodling. I have also become quite fond of fully stainless-steel frames.' Schooled in the art at the now legendary United Bicycle Institute in Ashland, Oregon, Alex focuses on creating hand-crafted bicycles that work well for the rider, 'things that are organically suited to a cyclist's goals, temperament and aesthetic sensibilities'.

His newest builds include a couple of cool fat bikes, built to be ridden over the roughest terrain or snow, and a stainless-steel city/tourer that leaves its builder nowhere to hide in terms of his welding skills. A-Train is no one-discipline specialist, and that's where Alex gets his kicks. Expect something different every time.

ESTABLISHED:	2008
LOCATION:	Minneapolis, Minnesota, USA
BIKE TYPE MADE:	Custom steel and stainless-steel frames and bikes
SPECIALITIES:	'Bikes and frame sets designed and hand-built for each rider, based upon his or her unique characteristics and riding style'
FAVOURITE RIDER:	'People with the passion to be part of a synergistic movement to broaden the appeal and redefine the vision of the bicycle'
FAVOURITE BICYCLE:	'My stainless-steel touring bike, seen here, now owned by Rod in Indianapolis'
FAVOURITE OBJECT:	The bicycle frame

BAUM CYCLES

Darren Baum was an A-grade cyclist until 1990, when he was involved in a car accident. Since then he has turned his attention, along with skills learned in the aircraft industry, to bike design and how bio-mechanics can be used to increase performance. 'When we weigh up all of the compromises that go into bike design, what is most important?' asks Darren. 'To make the lightest bike? The stiffest? Or the most beautiful? How about none of the above? The thing we're trying to do is build a bike that you will love to ride ten years from now.'

Having been mentored by master frame-builder Brian Cross, Darren has gone on to become a leader in his field. In 2010 he formed a research partnership with the Institute for Technical Research and Innovation at Deakin University in Australia to investigate sports applications for carbon-fibre and titanium. This quest for excellence is mirrored in his bike builds. All stages of manufacturing, from cad to tube-mitring, butting and painting, are completed in-house to ensure absolute control.

'In the final assembly, every bolt is torqued to manufacturer's specifications, cable ends soldered not crimped, bearings checked for alignment and smoothness, and each bicycle test-ridden and washed before it leaves the factory,' says Darren. 'Building bikes allows us to take an obsessive level of pride in our craft, because their scope is limited enough that it permits aiming for perfection. And even if we don't get there, we like that, too.'

ESTABLISHED:	1996
LOCATION:	North Shore, Victoria, Australia
BIKE TYPE MADE:	Hand-crafted titanium and steel bicycles
SPECIALITIES:	'Complete customization to suit each rider'
FAVOURITE RIDER:	Greg LeMond, Philippe Gilbert and Cadel Evans
FAVOURITE BICYCLE:	'Track bikes, with their classic lines, the most pure and connected form of cycling'
FAVOURITE OBJECT:	P-51 Mustang aircraft

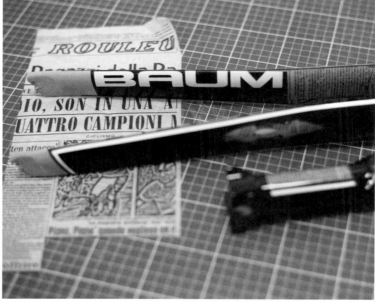

BELOVED CYCLES

'To feel the wind in your hair. To feel the sun on your face. To find new love for the neighbourhoods, the street corners, the passers-by. To reinspire the well-grooved commute. The freedom to find a new way. To wander. To work. To be among friends. Let us chase the sun.'

This is the inspirational edict emblazoned on the website of Beloved Cycles, a company founded by James Selman in 2009. Citing the French constructeur era as his own inspiration, James, who has been in the branding side of the cycle industry for over twenty years, has worked with such well-known frame-makers as Dave Levy (of Ti Cycles; pp. 250–1), Eric Estlund (Winter Bicycles; pp. 270–1), Chris King (Cielo Cycles; pp. 64–7) and currently Todd Gardner of Bronto Bikes to create classically styled bicycles under the Beloved name. 'After being around the bicycle industry for so many years,' he says, 'it was fun to be able to start a company from scratch that encompassed how I felt about riding, style, function and purity.'

James believes that the resurgence in hand-built, lugged steel-framed bicycles comes from a renewed sense of the importance of 'craft'. He sees the mounting interest in hauler-type models as proof of this, noting that people are not necessarily pushing for advanced materials, lighter bikes or high-tech solutions, but are instead looking back to a golden era of bicycles, while at the same time wanting to ride something practical yet cool. 'We strive to make everything about your bike, well, yours,' James says. 'How you want to use it, how you want to build it, how you envision it in colour, how you can't live without it.'

ESTABLISHED:	2009
LOCATION:	Portland, Oregon, USA
BIKE TYPE MADE:	French constructeur style, city and road
SPECIALITIES:	'Simple tried and true construction, inspired by the masters – solid colours, clean graphics, humble joy'
FAVOURITE RIDER:	All
FAVOURITE BICYCLE:	Any
FAVOURITE OBJECT:	Measuring tapes, rulers

BIKE BY ME

'Bike By Me ... the bike you like' is the antithesis of many of the bicycle artisans included within this book. But this Swedish firm is not to be ignored, because it is one of the leaders of an ever-growing industry in self-designed bicycles. You, the eventual owner, are put in charge of creating your very own design, from the colour of the chain set to the seat post, tyres and rims, frame and grips. The emphasis is on producing totally individual bikes at a lower cost than many of the traditional bicycle builders – a sort of mass marketing of the bespoke bike-building industry – hence some negativity from those who hand-build bikes from scratch.

The Bike By Me philosophy is different, and the results are cheerful, bright and extremely marketable. Those who want a bike simply go online and play around with the mix-and-match options until they have the 'bike they like', and then place an order. Bike By Me aims to ship most bikes within the week, and it will even accept returns within fourteen days if the customer doesn't, in the end, like the bike they ordered. This isn't bespoke bicycle design and manufacture, but it is an answer to the desire to be individual if your pockets aren't quite deep enough to commission the likes of Richard Schwinn to build a bike for you.

ESTABLISHED:	2009
LOCATION:	Stockholm, Sweden
PRODUCT:	Single-speed bikes
SPECIALITIES:	Fully customizable in colour, around 700,000 variations
FAVOURITE RIDER:	Lars Bengtsson
FAVOURITE BICYCLE:	The first
FAVOURITE OBJECT:	'Our own, of course!'

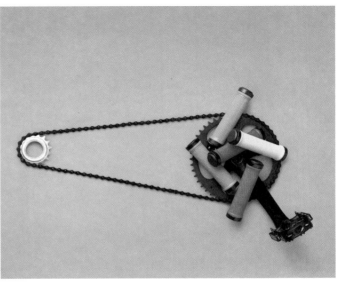

BISHOP BIKES

'I had been a bicycle courier since 1996 and riding bikes pretty much my whole life,' says Chris Bishop, owner of Maryland cycle-maker, Bishop Bikes. 'I owned a courier company and bike shop in the late 1990s/early 2000s, and had a mechanic, Matty, who took a frame-building course. Once he returned with a frame he had built, I knew I had to build one myself.'

Chris took the BREW and Yamaguchi frame-building classes, as well as the Serotta SICI size course, and became hooked on frame-building. He formed Bishop Bikes in 2007, and is now building about twenty bikes per year. Chris's influences have varied through-out his career, initially leaning towards the steel lugged Italian road and track bikes, which he spent a lot of time riding while working as a bicycle messenger, and today citing French constructeurs such as René Herse and Alex Singer, as well as the great American builders like Peter Johnson, Mark DiNucci and Peter Weigle, as his inspiration.

And inspiration, as well as passion, is what Chris believes leads people to want a custom-made bicycle. 'I think with so much out-sourcing of manufacturing and mass production, people miss and appreciate something that is built with care and quality in mind,' he says. 'A custom bike is one way that someone who is extremely passionate about bikes can manifest that love and, in the process, be rewarded with something that will provide continuing happiness.'

ESTABLISHED:	2007
LOCATION:	Baltimore, Maryland, USA
BIKE TYPE MADE:	Road, track/fixed, cyclocross, randonneur
SPECIALITIES:	Filleted lugs
FAVOURITE RIDER:	Mat Hoffman
FAVOURITE BICYCLE:	Peter Weigle rando
FAVOURITE OBJECT:	Buildings by Gaudí, furniture by Sam Maloof

BOHEMIAN BICYCLES

Bohemian Bicycles started out, much like many other bike-building ventures, in a rented garage. Dave Bohm, an artistic fellow with experience in silversmithing, wanted to create work with his hands: 'I am a certifiable bike nut, and I knew that I wanted to create tangible objects. The transition from silversmith to frame-builder was a logical one.'

Since founding Bohemian Bicycles in 1994, Dave has earned a reputation for creating some of the most beautiful custom steel bicycle frames in the world in his home-based workshop. 'Cyclists come to me looking for a unique, exquisitely crafted bicycle that they are proud to own and love to ride,' he says. 'What you end up with is a work of art that rides like a dream.'

Dave has taken his craft a step further, and has begun to teach budding frame-builders, too. His Bohemian Framebuilding School offers a two-week 'bike-building 101' course, which has students studying and living on-site in Tucson, while learning how to build their very own bicycle frames. 'You get the best instruction, the best facilities and the most beautiful weather (most of the time),' says Dave. 'But if you don't believe me, check out the frames that my students have created.'

ESTABLISHED:	1994
LOCATION:	Tucson, Arizona, USA
BIKE TYPE MADE:	Steel frames
SPECIALITIES:	Handmade lugs, jewelled frames, custom paint
FAVOURITE RIDER:	'Anybody actually riding their bike!'
FAVOURITE BICYCLE:	'That is like asking who is the prettiest woman in the world'
FAVOURITE OBJECT:	SR-71 'Blackbird'

BONDI BEACH CRUISERS

This relatively new bicycle maker entered the Australian market in 2011, with a laid-back pedal-powered cruiser aimed squarely at the beautiful young surfing crowd of Bondi Beach. It was the brainchild of Belinda Miller and Resa Pratoni, who together have spent years scouring garage sales, auctions and the Internet for vintage bicycles to restore and ride. 'After restoring a few bikes and receiving a lot of positive feedback,' says Resa, 'we set out to design our own bikes, and Bondi Beach Cruisers was born.'

It took about three months to come up with the design and refine the details: a classic beach-cruiser style, popular from the 1930s to the 1950s, with simple coaster breaks. Manufacturing began in 2010, and the first beach cruisers went on sale five months later to great public acclaim. 'Most of the bike industry is very focused on performance and technology,' says Resa. 'That sometimes can scare the average consumer from getting a bike. We need to be accessible to everyone, designing a bike with simplicity and comfort that looks fun to ride is a crucial part of our design.'

Resa believes that his and other makers' bikes will only get more popular, stating that cycling is the natural choice for people looking to find an economical and cool method of transportation. 'I also think that finding a boutique bicycle manufacturer or custom builder is a way to show the rider's personality,' he says. 'Hence the growing popularity in companies like ours.'

ESTABLISHED:	2011
LOCATION:	North Bondi, New South Wales, Australia
BIKE TYPE MADE:	Beach cruisers
SPECIALITIES:	Colours
FAVOURITE RIDER:	Anyone that has a bike
FAVOURITE BICYCLE:	Any vintage beach cruiser
FAVOURITE OBJECT:	Custom cruiser frames

BUSYMAN BICYLES

Not bicycle design but leather upholstery, which will elevate even the most mundane of fixies to most wanted in the bike rack – Busyman Bicycles is where those in the know go for a custom-made saddle. The company is owned and operated out of Melbourne, Australia, by Mick Peel, who used to work in fashion and has always had a penchant for leather. Today, he's turned his skills to designing and crafting beautiful, unique saddles for all types of bike.

'I start by making a pattern of the seat in fabric, transfer that reverse pattern to paper, and then plot the design and work up an upholstered leather saddle cover,' he explains. It all sounds so simple, but the exquisite quality of these bike seats are testament to the skill and craftsmanship that go into making each one. Mick works in a number of different hides: kid, cow, goat, even kangaroo, which he professes to be his favourite, 'for its combined strength and malleability'. His work is becoming more widely known, and in addition to keeping the fashion-conscious cyclists of Melbourne suitably stylish, Mick has created a diamanté-studded banana seat for a Middle Eastern customer and bespoke leather handlebar tape for US frame-builder and cycling legend Richard Sachs.

But ask Mick what he likes best about his work, and it's not the intricate designs or the interesting characters he meets. It is, he says, the way in which his designs age with wear and weather: 'They gain character, rather than looking worn out. They are graceful, changing with time, aging and maturing with their rider – often better than their rider!'

ESTABLISHED:	2008
LOCATION:	Melbourne, Victoria, Australia
BIKE TYPE MADE:	Bespoke hand-crafted leatherwork for bikes
SPECIALITIES:	Custom leather covers for bicycle saddles of all types, handlebar tape and tool bags/ rolls for high-end custom road bikes
FAVOURITE RIDER:	'Me!'
FAVOURITE BICYCLE:	Baum Corretto
FAVOURITE OBJECT:	The bicycle

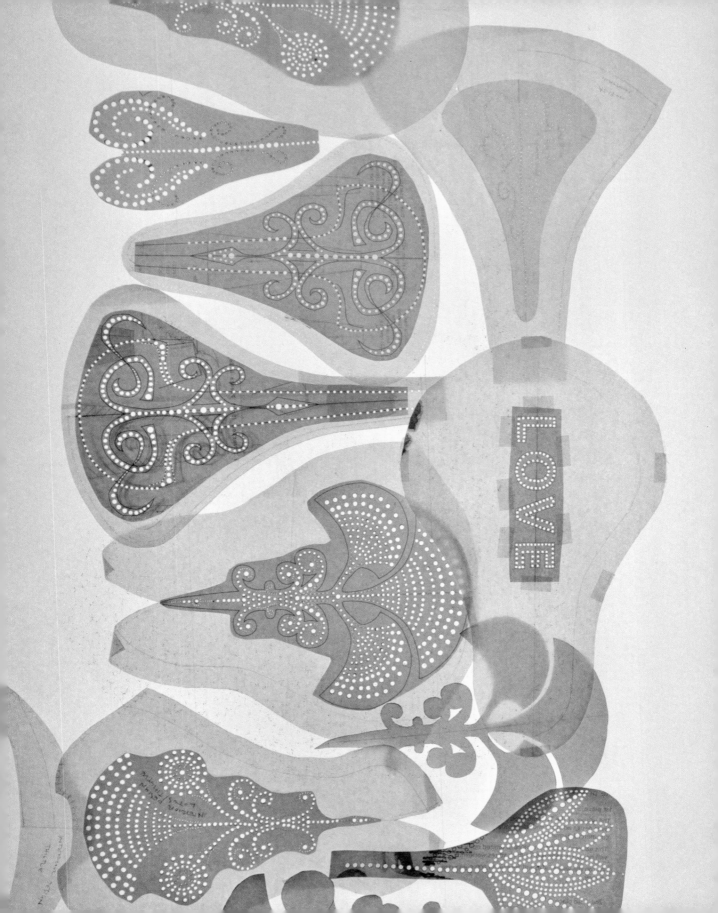

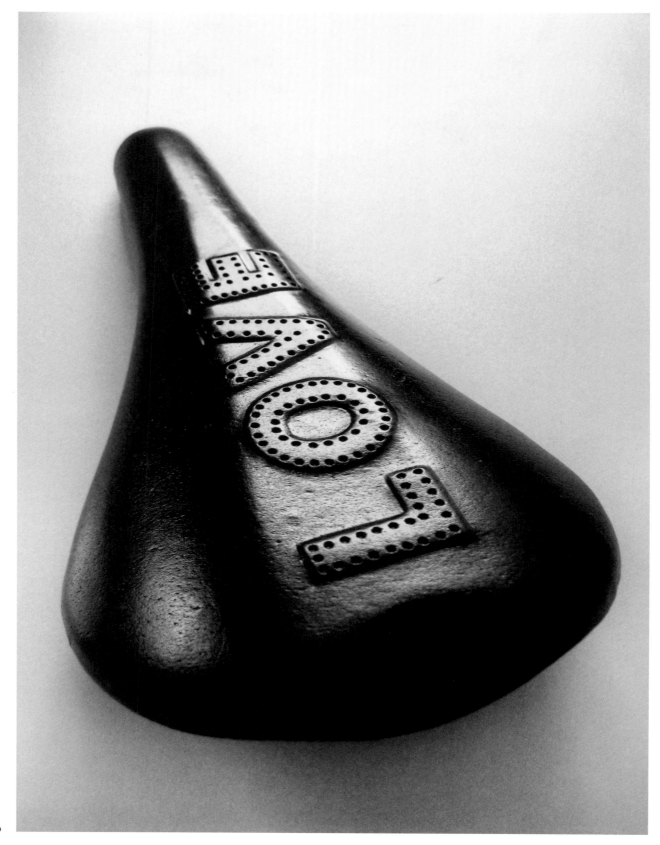

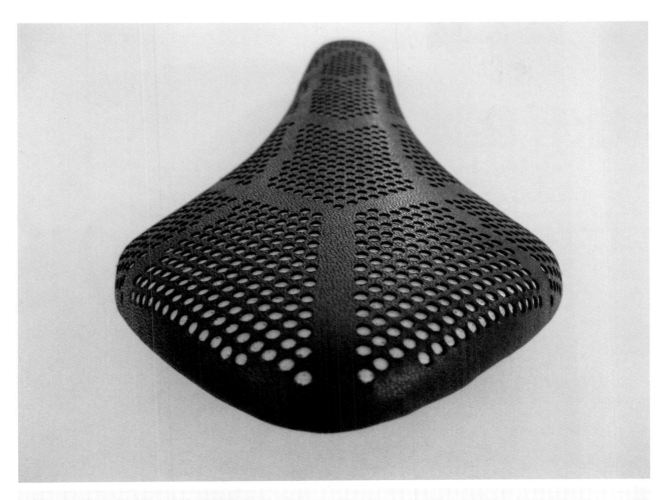

GARRETT CHOW

Garrett Chow doesn't make bikes – he isn't even trained as a welder – but he does have a huge influence in the cycling world. Garrett is a graphic designer who has made his name creating striking designs for bicycles, both as lead graphic designer for Specialized and for his own urban-cycling brand Mash. Garrett has been involved in the bike industry for a while now, first working for Wrench Science, a friend's bike shop, then Mash and now Specialized. He has also been an avid rider and street artist, and nowadays always makes time to spectate at the Tour de France, where the multitude of cyclists, advertising and fans provide plenty of inspiration. Combine these pursuits, and the influences behind his extravagant designs begin to come clear.

The philosophy behind Garrett's bike designs is one of creating a harmonious whole – bicycle and colour scheme working together to produce something special. 'In any possible scenario, a graphic design can make a bike look faster or lighter or more aggressive by sensitive and informed colour and graphics decisions,' he says. 'The graphic design should work in harmony with the design of the bicycle itself. If it battles against it or is not in tune, then neither the bike nor the graphic design will look good.'

Today Garrett's work is recognized worldwide. He has designed graphic art for bikes belonging to cyclocross star Zdeněk Štybar and two-time winner of the Tour de France, Alberto Contador. His work has even been featured in a one-man exhibition, *All the Chips on the Table: The Bicycle Art and Design of Garrett Chow*, held at the Rapha Cycle Club in San Francisco in 2012.

LOCATION:	Morgan Hill, California, USA
BIKE TYPE MADE:	'What's your flavour?!'
FAVOURITE RIDER:	Roger De Vlaeminck
FAVOURITE BICYCLE:	The original, Pesenti-built Cinelli Laser aero-track
FAVOURITE OBJECT:	Millau Viaduct by Foster + Partners

CICLI MAESTRO

What do Leonardo da Vinci and 1950s track bikes have in common? Not much to most people, but a lot to the guys at Cicli Maestro. Taking their inspiration from the art and architecture that is all around them at their base in Milan, the design team for this bicycle-maker has utilized Da Vinci's *Uomo Vitruviano* – the graphic representation of the human body's perfect proportions – in their logo. But more than that, they found that the Golden Ratio (1.618:1) is the perfect proportional measurement between a cyclist's leg length and the ideal frame size or the seat tube. Coincidence? Probably not.

The team's next step was to take original designs from steel track bikes of the 1950s and '60s, and offer customers the chance to custom-build their own perfect bicycle. 'We wanted to take the idea of mass-customization into bikes, a market that so far has only seen either very expensive or mass-produced products,' the designers explain. 'In a world where people look to be different from everybody else, the chance to decide about colours and components of a bicycle should be offered, don't you think?'

The track-frame designs have been modified slightly for road use, but steel is still the material of choice because the designers believe in its strength and longevity. Cicli Maestro's selling point is that it is the only company offering a made-in-Italy, customizable bicycle that customers can tailor to suit their needs by choosing between half a million different combinations.

ESTABLISHED:	2011
LOCATION:	Milan, Italy
PRODUCT:	Steel frame, leather saddles, handmade assembled wheels for single-speed bikes
SPECIALITIES:	'We combine traditional bike-building with a modern way of interacting with our customers to help their creativity'
FAVOURITE RIDER:	Fausto Coppi
FAVOURITE BICYCLE:	Coppi's Bianchi
FAVOURITE OBJECT:	1970s Porsche 911

CIELO CYCLES

Cielo Cycles is named after Camino Cielo, a narrow road that clings to a high ridge in the Santa Ynez Mountains near Santa Barbara, California. Described as 'a rugged and adventurous road' by master bicycle-maker Chris King, its climbs, twists, turns and speedy descents inspired the name for his company, which he formed in 1978, mothballed in the early 1980s and resurrected in 2008.

Chris is renowned for his manufacturing company, Chris King Precision Components, but his first love was frame-building. Initially building racing and touring frames, he soon got noticed and began to work for racing teams, as well as individual clients, from his small shop in Santa Barbara. He also produced mountain bikes, and the sport was quick to appreciate his sealed bearing headset design. Having moved away from frame-building to concentrate on his component business, Chris stepped back into the arena in 2008, following many conversations with fellow bike-builders and seeing that the demand for custom-built steel frames was on the rise.

Today, Cielo Cycles is one of the most respected bicycle-makers in Portland and beyond, and Chris is once again doing what he loved forty years ago. And if he needs any reminding of why he's frame-building once again, he need look no further than the engraved brass head tube badge on every bicycle that he produces. It features La Cumbre Peak, the highest ridge in the Santa Ynez mountain range – a reminder of past conquests and a source of inspiration for future achievements.

ESTABLISHED:	1978
LOCATION:	Portland, Oregon, USA
BIKE TYPE MADE:	Headsets, hubs and bottom brackets
FAVOURITE OBJECT:	Bearings

CIRCLE A CYCLES

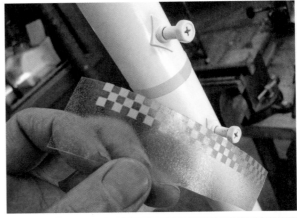

'A frame from us is more than your transportation, it's your companion on adventures. It will listen when no one else will. It won't judge. It knows how to get you home safely. It offers good advice and knows how to make a strong cup of coffee or a stronger mint julep.'

This somewhat left-field statement from Circle A Cycles is indicative of the subversive nature of the company's co-owners, Chris Bull and Brian Chapman. The duo specialize in custom steel frames, lugged, TIG-welded and fillet-brazed, frame repairs and repaints, and, in their spare time, 'smashing the state'. The company philosophy has more to do with building and riding bikes than it does with making money, and focuses on looking at the industry from an environmental ideal. For instance, the choice of steel over aluminium or titanium as a frame material is due to its lower production cost, ease of handling and recyclability. The guys also insist that they prefer to build bikes for bicycle lovers, rather than for wealthy collectors. They repair bikes for kids, and show the same kids how to maintain them.

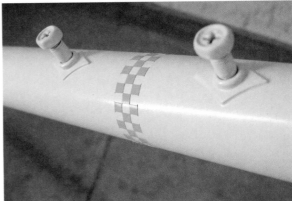

Circle A Cycles is a bike-building firm for all budding socialists, and for anyone else who wants a bike built with the right intentions. 'For us, bikes aren't toys or simple transportation or art,' say Chris and Brian. 'They represent a human-scaled and powered future. They are the revolution.'

ESTABLISHED:	2001
LOCATION:	Providence, Rhode Island, USA
BIKE TYPE MADE:	Custom steel frames and forks
SPECIALITIES:	Rando bikes with integrated lighting, belt drives, fixed-gear commuters
FAVOURITE RIDER:	'Don't really have one'
FAVOURITE BICYCLE:	'We love designs from the 1890s and 1900s, which were pushing the limits of the materials available at the time'
FAVOURITE OBJECT:	Rolleiflex cameras, Lotus Super Seven sports car

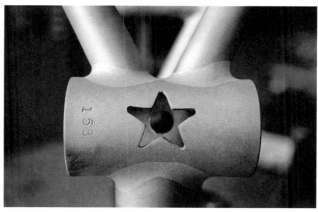

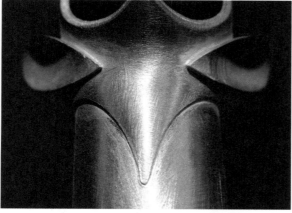

COAST CYCLES

'Beautiful, classic, true to the process' is the mantra of Johnny Coast, owner of Coast Cycles and a bicycle builder who, while admitting to city bikes as being some of his favourite creations, can't help but show off his beautifully crafted tourers. Johnny is adamant that he's not interested in a pre-fab, one-size-fits-all, disposable culture, or in bikes that are built for our throwaway society.

'I'm building quality frames that will last your lifetime,' he says, 'using the same techniques that master builders of high-end bicycles have used for ages.' As if to prove a point, Johnny alludes to his schooling in stem design and building under master frame-builder Koichi Yamaguchi at the Yamaguchi frame-building school, along with qualifications from the United Bicycle Institute in Oregon for brazing and lugged construction: 'I can design custom stems for your frame – a standard 1-in. [2.5 cm] quill stem with a classic look, built using newer technologies.'

Johnny builds frames one at a time in his small workshop. Each hand-built silver-brazed frame is tailored to suit its rider's needs, type of riding and body shape. He stakes his reputation on his skills: 'Instead of trying to fit your body to an already existing bike, I will design your frame to meet the dimensions of your body. It's easy to make a bike that is merely rideable, but it takes talent, skill and craftsmanship to make a bike that only you can truly ride.'

ESTABLISHED:	2005
LOCATION:	Brooklyn, New York, USA
BIKE TYPE MADE:	Custom silver-brazed frames and forks; fillet-brazed racks, stems and decalures
SPECIALITIES:	Randonneuring, touring and road bikes
FAVOURITE RIDER:	George – 'he's sixty-four, and has been commuting by bicycle in New York City for thirty-five years'
FAVOURITE BICYCLE:	René Herse randonneuring bicycles
FAVOURITE OBJECT:	'The bicycle itself! The tools that make them! From the milling machine and lathe in my shop, right down to the files'

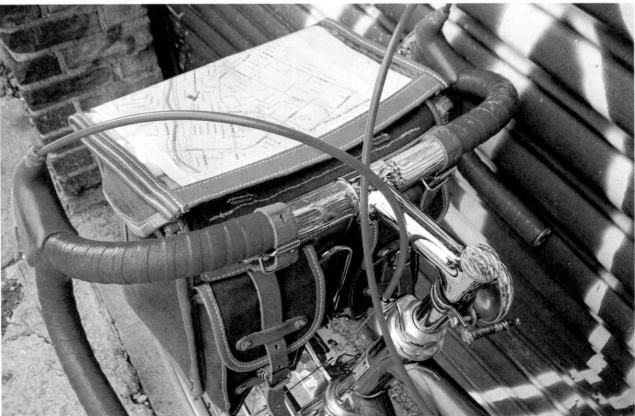

COLUMBINE CYCLE WORKS

Columbine Cycle Works gets its name from a flower found in high-altitude woods and meadows in the Northern Hemisphere. The reason for naming a bicycle company after a flower? 'The columbine's colour, stature and beauty are stunning,' says co-founder John Murphy, who together with his brother Richard set up the firm in 1979. 'It became the symbol for the quality and special character found in every frame we produce.'

Columbine's evolution is a familiar tale in the bike-building world. 'An idea became a hobby, a hobby became an obsession, an obsession a way of life,' says John. The brothers' goal was to produce some of the finest bicycles in the world, and their designs certainly stand out among all the other cookie-cutter styling as statements of individuality and personal expression.

The company makes a variety of bikes, from road racing and cyclocross/hybrid to extreme mountain bikes. 'While factory-produced frames must be nailed down to narrow specifications,' says John, 'Columbine frames do not need that type of conformity.' And every aspect of the design is custom-designed and built: 'You will receive the best performance with the least compromise. Our bikes are that rare exception in life, where you can have your cake and eat it, too!'

ESTABLISHED:	1979
LOCATION:	Mendocino, California, USA
BIKE TYPE MADE:	Lightweight frames and handlebar stems for road, cyclocross/hybrid, touring and mountain bikes, occasional track frames
SPECIALITIES:	Stainless-steel lugwork, lug-relief carving
FAVOURITE RIDER:	Eddy Merckx
FAVOURITE BICYCLE:	'Everyday ultra-light hybrid that can go anywhere, fast'

CONCEPT BIKES

Bicycle design is always evolving – sometimes dramatically, taking on an entirely new form, and sometimes gradually, as riders push the boundaries of one discipline or morph it into another. This is precisely what has happened with the BMX bike in recent years. Riders like the freestyle ideal but they also want better all-round ridability, so the fixed-gear freestyle bike was born.

Concept Bikes was the first Canadian company to design and produce a fixed-gear freestyle bike, with founder Jason McBain and his crew some of the best riders of these new machines. 'The original idea was that riding a fixed-gear track bike with no brakes was crazy hard,' says Jason, 'so anything you did on it in terms of tricks was considered pretty cool. Things have grown rapidly from there. At Concept, we are innovators in the sport and are pushing the direction of possibility.'

Having only been formed in 2012, in its first year the company has produced over five hundred frames and forks. Jason comes from an engineering background, but his passion for riding spurred him on to make Concept his primary career. 'The main influence on my design is a combination of my road and mountain-bike backgrounds, as well as experience in design engineering and working with and riding steel bikes,' he says. 'That, and riding every day for the last twenty-five years.'

ESTABLISHED:	2012
LOCATION:	Burnaby, British Columbia, Canada
BIKE TYPE MADE:	Fixed-gear freestyle
SPECIALITIES:	Unique chain-stay yoke, and cutting-edge geometry
FAVOURITE RIDER:	Eddy Merckx
FAVOURITE BICYCLE:	The first Columbus MAX frame sets
FAVOURITE OBJECT:	Buckminster Fuller's geodesic dome

CORIMA

Corima, founded in 1973 by Pierre Martin and Jean-Marie Riffard, is a company that is expert in the production of mechanical moulding: the making of moulds and models for the foundry, automotive and aeronautics sectors. In 1988, it diversified into the production of carbon composite parts and launched its first product for the cycling sector, the Disc wheel, which was followed by numerous other parts that have expanded into a full range of carbon products for cycling.

Owing to the company's experience in working with composite materials, Corima controls all of the steps in the manufacturing process, from design and production to control and after-sales service at its plant in Loriol-sur-Drôme in south-eastern France. Its wheels are used by cycling teams worldwide – from its monobloc Disc wheels, first designed in 1988, to the new twelve-spoked MCC wheels, all have been ridden by champion cyclists. Corima currently supplies wheels to the Astana Pro Team, whose team leader Alexander Vinokourov won the gold medal in the Men's Road Race at the London 2012 Summer Olympics.

Corima uses high-performance carbon-fibre to provide their Aero+ MCC carbon wheels with rotational inertia without sacrificing strength. A new carbon-fibre layering technique enables the team to build the wheels with the minimum number of spokes for improved aerodynamics and lateral stiffness. The company claims that the exceptional quality of these carbon spokes reduces ground drift while riding and improves performance – feeling light when climbing, faster on flat roads and more responsive in the sprints.

ESTABLISHED:	1973
LOCATION:	Loriol-sur-Drôme, France
PRODUCT:	Carbon wheels and carbon track frame
SPECIALITIES:	Manufacturing technical, top-performance products, including the Aero+ MCC and Viva MCC 'S' wheels
FAVOURITE RIDER:	Astana Pro Team – 'the team we sponsor!'
FAVOURITE BICYCLE:	Corima Puma road frame
FAVOURITE OBJECT:	Aero+ MCC wheels and V.I.F. track frame

DESALVO CUSTOM CYCLES

In 1985 the 7-Eleven Cycling Team visited twelve-year-old Mike DeSalvo's hometown – an event that inspired him to get a job in a local bike store. It was, he says, the moment that shaped his career. Today, Mike is considered by his peers to be one of the best welders in the bike-building business. But things are never that simple: it wasn't until 1999 that Mike built his first frame, and 2001 before the hobby turned into a full-time job. In the meantime, Mike had graduated from a frame-building course at the United Bicycle Institute in Ashland, Oregon, taken it easy in Colorado for a few years, and then returned to southern Oregon to teach at UBI, where he continues to teach today.

Mike now builds about 120 frames a year, varying between road, cyclocross and mountain bikes. His custom cyclocross bikes are renowned the world over, and are ridden by the likes of Barry Wicks and Carl Decker. TIG-welded titanium frames are a favourite, and Mike cites his gravel road bikes as the fastest-growing sector of client requests. Fans and peers alike always look for Mike on the winner's rostrum at the North American Handmade Bicycle Show, where he has won trophies in 2005, 2006, 2008 and 2010.

ESTABLISHED:	1999
LOCATION:	Ashland, Oregon, USA
BIKE TYPE MADE:	Steel and titanium frames
SPECIALITIES:	Road, single-speed, cyclocross and mountain bikes
FAVOURITE RIDER:	Andrew Hampsten
FAVOURITE BICYCLE:	Eddy Merckx
FAVOURITE OBJECT:	Vintage Italian motorcycles

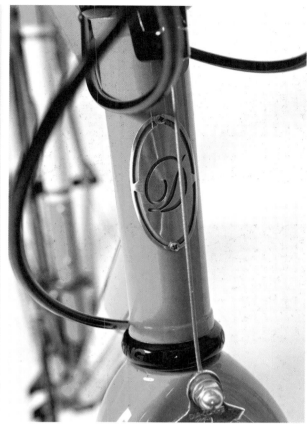

DETROIT BICYCLE COMPANY

Like many bicycle artisans, Steven Bock came to the industry via another discipline, and it took time and experimentation to find his true calling. Steven is a veteran of the design industry, and began his career creating custom furniture, later working as a concept-car builder and clay modeller in the automotive sector. All the while, he remained an avid amateur cyclist, and crafted bicycles in his spare time. In 2010, he formed the Detroit Bicycle Company.

Steven's hand-crafted designs are inspired by the track bikes of the 1930s. His latest creation is the copper-plated Madison Street, which encompasses a quirky blend of vintage-era parts and classic lines. Clients can choose from three standard frame sizes, built to order in his studio, or have a frame customized to their exact specifications. All frames are made with Columbus SL cro-mo tubing and Nova lugs, and the company offers a number of combinations of materials and finishes, including painted, steel and chrome, among others.

'The company's design aesthetic can be described as historical with modern twists,' says Steven. 'We hand-craft each bicycle to order, and because of our experience in other design fields, our attention to design and detail is world class.'

ESTABLISHED:	2010
LOCATION:	Detroit, Michigan, USA
BIKE TYPE MADE:	Custom bespoke bicycles
SPECIALITIES:	Single-speed bikes with unique finishes
FAVOURITE RIDER:	'Major' Taylor, Mat Hoffman
FAVOURITE BICYCLE:	Pre-war Schwinn Paramount track bikes

TORKEL DOHMERS

Swedish product and industrial designer Torkel Dohmers is just one of a number of entrants in this book who do not build bicycles for a living. But like the other non-specialists, Torkel, a graduate of London's Royal College of Art and winner of many international design competitions, was attracted to bike design by the potential for bringing something completely different to the table.

Torkel's ThisWay bicycle, designed for and winner of Bicycle Design's 'Commuter bike for the masses' competition, is a recumbent with a difference. It is a two-speed, carbon-fibre/aluminium design, weighing just 12kg (26 lbs), and features LED lights, front and rear, powered by a roof-mounted solar panel, and belt-drive propulsion hidden within the composite frame. Most noticeable, however, is the overarching roof, which stretches like an elongated visor right over the rider. Torkel admits that there are already roofed bicycles on the market, but insists that ThisWay is more buyer-friendly, being both a covetable design and more open to the environment than the current models for human-powered vehicles or velomobiles.

'ThisWay is my proposal for a feasible design, which I believe has the potential to become a commercial product and to get more people interested in commuting by bike,' Torkel says. 'It's a bike with a roof for weather protection, something we can all appreciate in Northern Europe.'

ESTABLISHED:	2001
LOCATION:	Stockholm, Sweden
BIKE TYPE MADE:	Track frames, commuters, bespoke bikes
SPECIALITIES:	'Conceptual design, from ideas and sketches to digital prototypes, for product, transportation, interior and exhibition design'
FAVOURITE BICYCLE:	Cinelli Laser and Itera
FAVOURITE OBJECT:	Bertone Stratos concept car

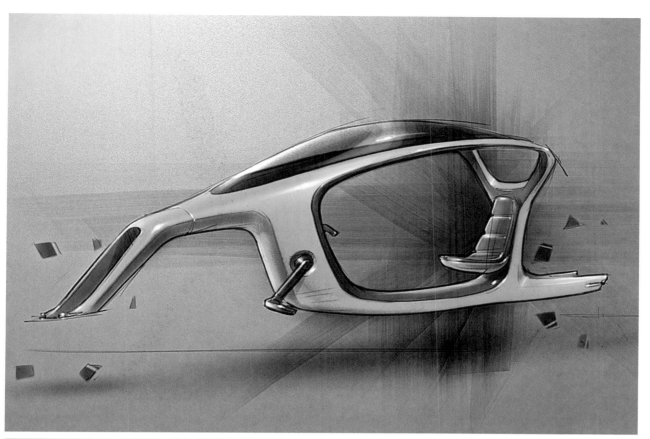

DONHOU BICYCLES

It takes time to work out your vocation in life, and for Thomas Donhou, it was no different. After childhood and teenage years spent riding BMX, recumbent, racing and mountain bikes, Thomas went to university and then on a road trip that included cycling across the Gobi Desert. 'It took until that point in northern China, as I lay in my tent at the side of the road being kept awake by coal trucks rumbling endlessly past, to realize what I wanted to do,' he says. 'Kind of like when you realize that the cute girl you've grown up with you actually love, I realized that I absolutely needed to start making bikes. It couldn't have been any clearer.'

At his workshop in East London, Thomas builds all his bicycles in-house, one at a time. 'From picking, cutting and shaping the tubes to the final coat of paint, it is a full custom build and experience. Every detail is thought through to make sure the client receives a perfect bike in terms of aesthetics, fit and ride,' he says. Thomas likes his customers to be involved in the process, as riding is about the experience – and, at Donhou, so is the building. 'We use traditional methods,' he says, 'but we're not afraid to throw in a few modern ones in order to build the most beautiful bicycles. They're built with the foundations of clear thinking and a love for working with the customer, as well as a design process in which your dream bicycle is translated from mind to physical being.'

ESTABLISHED:	2009
LOCATION:	Hackney, London, UK
BIKE TYPE MADE:	Frames/complete bikes
SPECIALITIES:	Using traditional methods in a contemporary, design-led way
FAVOURITE RIDER:	Burt Munro
FAVOURITE BICYCLE:	'Any bike that's seen some miles or gone fast'
FAVOURITE OBJECT:	'The pushbike, of course!'

ELLIS CYCLES

'I always had a bike growing up, cruising around the neighbourhood, seeing who could skid the farthest,' says Dave Wages, owner of Ellis Cycles. 'But I didn't truly get hooked until my twelfth birthday when I received a silver Raleigh Record ten-speed. The kids' bike I had been riding wasn't cutting it on the hills around our house, and suddenly I had the ability to get up all those hills and see the countryside. I've never looked back.'

A succession of bike-shop jobs led to Dave's big chance. In 1994 he got a job at Serotta, and was soon under the tutelage of Dave Kirk. Waterford Precision Cycles came next (another lugged-steel frame-maker), and in 2008 Ellis Cycles was born. 'With a leap of faith, a 500-lb alignment table, some oxyacetylene tanks and the help of a handful of good friends, I started building frames,' he says. A year after founding the company, an Ellis 953 frame was awarded Best Lugged Bike at the North American Handmade Bicycle Show: 'Quite an honour, considering the collection of talent there,' Dave recalls.

Since then, Dave has been refining his craft, building beautiful lugged steel-framed bicycles. He has won Best in Show and Best Steel Frame at the NAHBS three years running in 2010, 2011 and 2012. So what's the secret? 'Well thought-out geometries, the ideal choice of tubing for each rider's needs, immaculate brazing and finish work, frames that are aligned straight and true and built for the long haul,' says Dave. 'Yes, the end product is stunning, but the beauty is integral, functional – more than just a shiny head badge.'

ESTABLISHED:	2008
LOCATION:	Waterford, Wisconsin, USA
BIKE TYPE MADE:	Steel frames, forks and complete bikes
SPECIALITIES:	'I do quite a bit with polished stainless tubing and lugs'
FAVOURITE RIDER:	Sean Kelly
FAVOURITE BICYCLE:	'Any that's being ridden hard!'
FAVOURITE OBJECT:	'I am pretty hooked on the Shimano Di2'

ENGIN CYCLES

'A love of the bicycle is at the heart and soul of Engin Cycles,' says Drew Guldalian, the company's designer and builder. 'Our mission is to build bicycles that appeal to people both as a work of craft and as a machine that can be ridden, and ridden often.' Drew goes on to explain that there is more to an Engin bicycle than is immediately apparent, citing the many subtle, sometimes hidden touches and features that go into the end result. 'The process is very much part of the product,' he says, 'and this is where so much time and energy has been invested.'

Each of Engin's bicycles is built one at a time, with a specific rider in mind: people are different, so each frame is different. Design, fit, tubes, construction method and aesthetics are all taken into consideration when building the perfect bicycle for each client. 'If you choose to have us build your new bicycle, our passion for the craft and sport will be apparent in every detail, and you will have the pleasure of riding a bicycle that is unique to you,' Drew says.

The company TIG-welds, fillet-brazes and custom-makes lugs. Steel is the material most often used to build frames, but as of 2013 Engin also offers titanium frames. 'If you browse our online gallery, you will see that this versatility allows us to mix methods and materials and to utilize different types of construction to our, and your, advantage,' Drew explains. 'We feel our process is strong and effective, and always takes you, the end user, into consideration.'

ESTABLISHED:	2005
LOCATION:	Philadelphia, Pennsylvania, USA
BIKE TYPE MADE:	Steel and titanium frames, stems and seat posts, steel forks
SPECIALITIES:	Each product is tailor-made to order
FAVOURITE RIDER:	'The rider having the most fun with a bicycle I made is my favourite – professional riders are not my inspiration'
FAVOURITE BICYCLE:	The first safety bicycle – 'to have come up with that first design and concept over a high-wheeler is very clever'
FAVOURITE OBJECT:	Bridges – 'both how they are made and what they do'

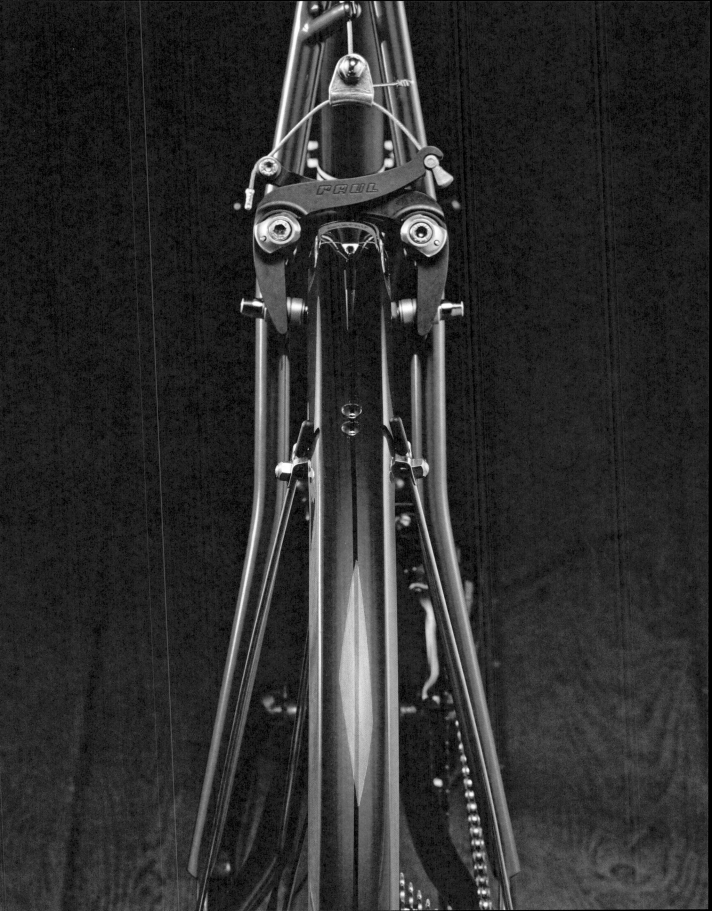

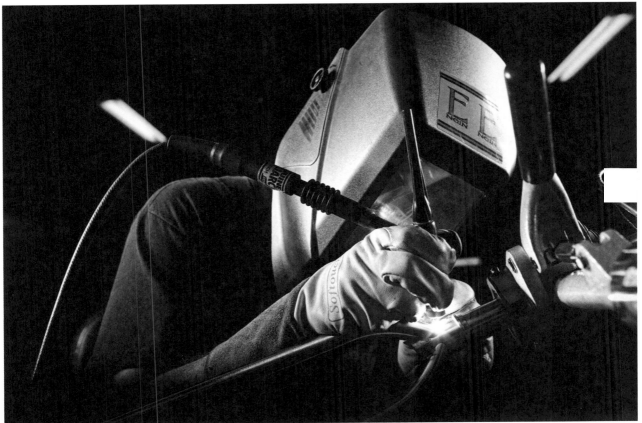

ENIGMA BIKES

An eleventh-century village on England's south coast is not where you would expect to find a bicycle-maker who is crafting some of the leading lightweight bikes in the world, but this is exactly where you will find Enigma Bikes. 'Britain's heritage for bicycle building is as old as the bicycle itself,' says master frame-builder Jim Walker, 'but sadly, over the last few decades, almost all bicycle manufacturing in the UK has disappeared. Enigma is passionate about and committed to the frame-builder's art, and all of our bespoke frames are made by us, by hand, right here in rural Sussex, within an easy Mark Cavendish-sprint of the oldest Norman church in England.'

Jim and the team believe that the frame is the heart and soul of any bike: 'Components come and go, but the frame is the frame and has to be perfect right from the start.' All of Enigma's frames, made in their workshop and shipped to customers across the globe, are made from the finest seamless titanium or the lightest, strongest grades of space-age steel – materials that not only give the bicycles a timeless grace and elegance, but also offer genuine competitive alternatives to carbon-fibre when it comes to making high-end bicycles that meet the demands of today's riders.

'There is no production line here, and no shortcuts taken,' says Jim. 'Each length of tubing is individually selected, precision-cut, mitred, then fitted together by a master frame-builder with a legacy of thousands of frames behind him. No detail is too small, from the rider's measurements to the scrutiny of the raw tubing at the start of the build to the impeccable finish at the end.'

ESTABLISHED:	2006
LOCATION:	Hailsham, East Sussex, UK
BIKE TYPE MADE:	Frames
SPECIALITIES:	Titanium frames and finishes
FAVOURITE RIDER:	Bradley Wiggins
FAVOURITE BICYCLE:	Pegoretti
FAVOURITE OBJECT:	Burj Khalifa – 'that tower in Dubai, the tallest building in the world'

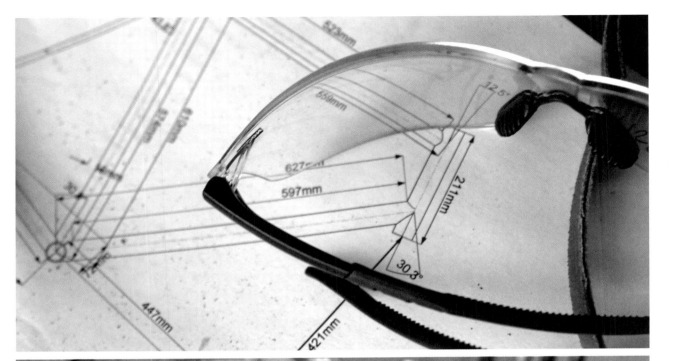

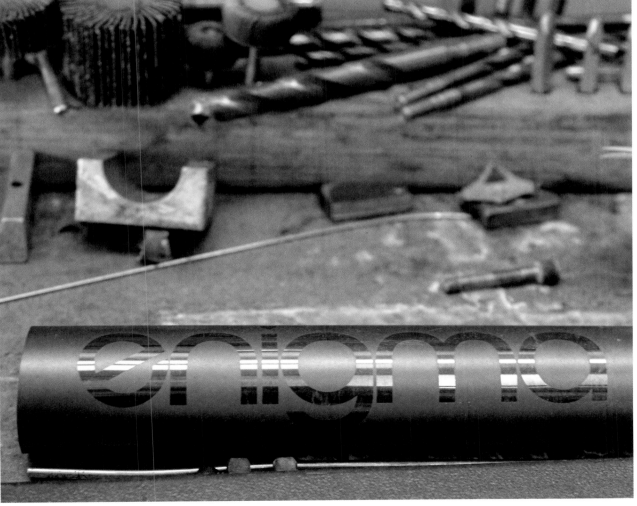

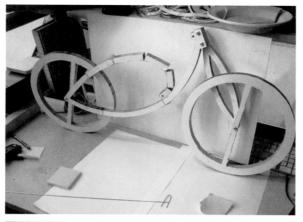

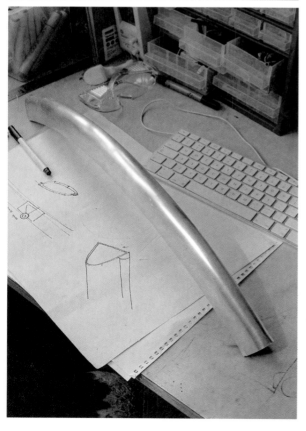

EYE TO HAND

As the head of multidisciplinary design studio Eye To Hand, Dominic Hargreaves tackles all kinds of projects, from digital media to industrial design. Following an undergraduate degree at Ravensbourne College of Design and Communication, he moved on to the Royal College of Art to study Design Products – a discipline that has proved particularly useful as the company has collaborated with many big names in the product-design world, including Nike, Jaguar, Land Rover, 3 Mobile and Lunartik.

Recently, Dominic shot to the attention of the cycling world with his design for a folding bicycle, the Contortionist. A neat, foldable design that incorporates full-size wheels has long been the Holy Grail of the folding-bicycle fraternity, and while there are now a few on the market, designers are still pushing to create one that rivals its non-folding counterparts in terms of both looks and ridability. This is where Dominic has come good. The Contortionist's wheels are attached to offset single forks, rather than sets of two, and are slightly misaligned to aid folding. The aluminium frame folds to smaller than the diameter of the wheels, which are used to roll the folded bike. Pedals power a hydraulic system, set within the frame, to turn the rear wheel. The result is no chain, leaving clothes oil-free when the folded bike is carried or lifted.

'It is a bike that folds, rather than a folding bike,' Dominic says. 'That was my initial aim for the project.'

ESTABLISHED:	2005
LOCATION:	London, UK
BIKE TYPE MADE:	Aluminium folding bike
SPECIALITIES:	'Creating designs that take new approaches to the way we do things'
FAVOURITE RIDER:	Steve Peat
FAVOURITE BICYCLE:	Alex Moulton's SPEED
FAVOURITE OBJECT:	Britten V1000 motorcycle by John Britten – 'it made the impossible happen'

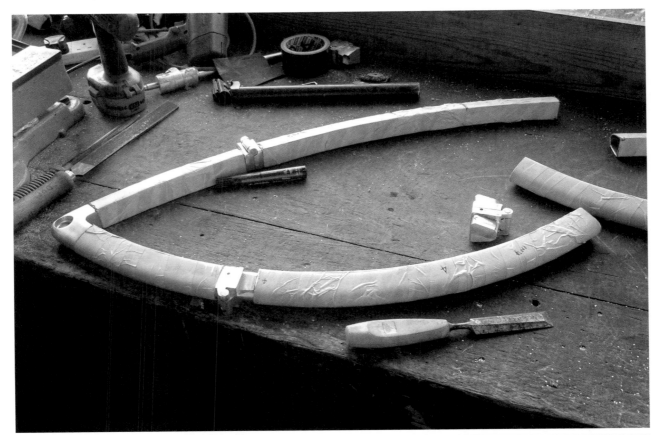

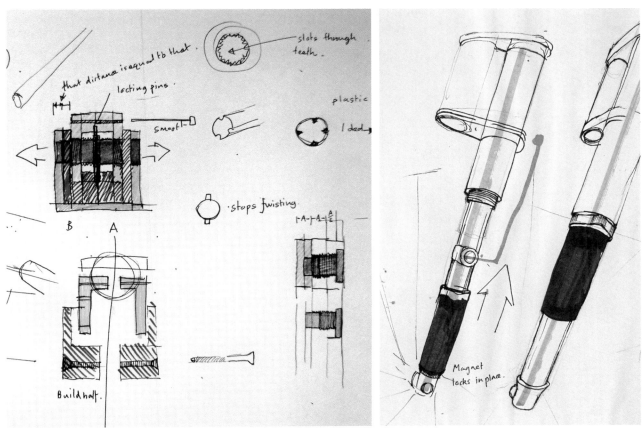

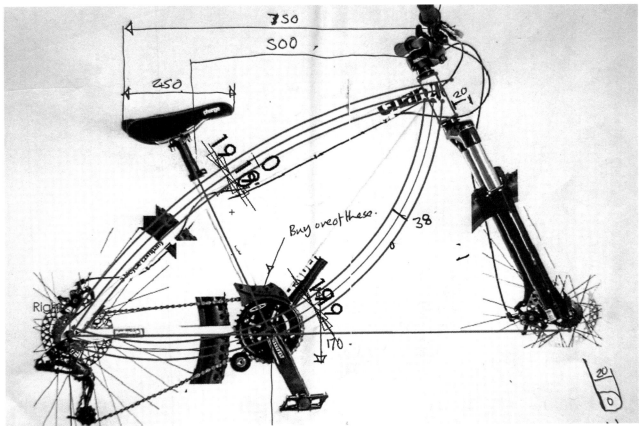

FARADAY BICYCLES

While the majority of bicycles in this book are made by single companies, a few are collaborations, and the Faraday bicycle, named after the scientist Michael Faraday, whose work in electromagnetism helped pave the way for today's safe electric motors, is the result of one such fruitful pairing. This utility bike was designed and built by a team of designers from IDEO and Paul Sadoff of Rock Lobster Cycles (pp. 204–5) for Oregon Manifest, and is now in production under the brand Faraday Bicycles.

Among the aims of the Oregon Manifest event is the promotion of the utility bike as a transportation mode of the future for those who want to live healthier, more sustainable lives, but who don't necessarily think of themselves as cyclists. The Faraday has an integrated electric hub motor and custom cycle computer for seamless electric-pedal assist. The bike also has a quick-release front-rack mechanism that can accommodate a variety of cargo-carrying accessories, as well as built-in front and rear lights with ambient light sensing, a handmade leather bag and grips and fenders made from steam-bent ash.

With the Faraday, the team sought to capture the advantages that an electric-assist utility bicycle might bring to a (very) hilly city like San Francisco, while overcoming many of the drawbacks that can hamper existing e-bike designs. Everything from the bike's electronics to its controls have been created to disappear into the design, which can be described as classic with a modern twist. 'We drew inspiration from both history and our own childhoods to create an everyday performance bicycle,' says IDEO's Adam Vollmer. 'Our mantra is, "You loved bicycling when you were a kid, so why stop?"'

ESTABLISHED:	2012
LOCATION:	San Francisco, California, USA
BIKE TYPE MADE:	Electric city bicycles
FAVOURITE RIDER:	Albert Einstein
FAVOURITE BICYCLE:	Pegoretti Marcelo
FAVOURITE OBJECT:	Tesla Roadster

ALEX FERNÁNDEZ CAMPS

Understanding the way an object works at human scale is how Spanish industrial designer Alex Fernández Camps approaches each of his projects, whether bicycles, lighting or furniture. 'Instead of working from the object, I work from people and situations,' he explains, 'and then I try to compose the piece in the simplest way possible.'

Grow is Alex's solution to the age-old problem of children outgrowing their bicycles too quickly. The design has a lightweight aluminium frame with an adjustable seat and handlebars, but it differs from other models in that the frame length is also adjustable. 'Because the bicycle grows in size, it can be used by the same child for twice the time – one bike, instead of two or more,' Alex says. 'The other advantage of Grow, apart from reduced economical and eco-logical costs throughout the whole of its life cycle, is a much better ergonomic adjustment for the user. Kids often ride a too small or too big bike for quite a long time, which is not healthy.'

Alex's simple and intuitive adaptation of the conventional child's bike comes from his alternative approach to the challenge. Grow is the third iteration from the Orbea series of kids' bicycles, which also includes a runner bike (with no pedals) for toddlers and a chain-driven model without an adjustable frame.

ESTABLISHED:	2004
LOCATION:	Barcelona, Spain
BIKE TYPE MADE:	Kids' bikes
SPECIALITIES:	'Growing' bikes
FAVOURITE RIDER:	'All of us!'
FAVOURITE BICYCLE:	The Rover (1860) – 'one of the first industrial-produced bicycles'
FAVOURITE OBJECT:	The paper clip

FIREFLY BICYCLES

Jamie Medeiros, Tyler Evans and Kevin Wolfson have brought together over thirty years of frame-building experience, as well as a degree in neuroscience, a background in graphic design and a penchant for creating 'nerdy little devices designed to take over the world' to form the team behind Firefly Bicycles. The trio are based in Boston, Massachusetts, one of the hubs of the handmade bike-building scene. They are all serious cyclists, too (with Kevin leading the way, competing in Category 1 races across North America), and are dedicated to making high-performance, road, cyclocross and mountain bikes in stainless steel and titanium.

Since leaving a career as a bicycle messenger in 1993, Jamie has worked on all aspects of the frame-building process, from making tools to streamlining production processes and developing prototypes and world-renowned concept bikes. Tyler, meanwhile, has concentrated on frame-building over the course of his fifteen years in the business, and his tally to date amounts to over 10,000 frames welded. Kevin embarked upon a career in custom frame design after receiving a BA in neuroscience, which may seem strange, but he grew up in a family of avid cyclists and has been riding since before he could walk. In the last three years, he has designed over 1,200 custom frames.

'Firefly was born because we love our craft,' explains Jamie. 'We know our clients appreciate the intelligence, passion, meticulous attention to detail and quality materials that go into every frame we make.'

ESTABLISHED:	2011
LOCATION:	Boston, Massachusetts, USA
BIKE TYPE MADE:	Custom titanium or stainless-steel road, mountain, cyclocross, track, touring and commuter bikes
SPECIALITIES:	Raw titanium finishes, including bead-blasted, brushed, polished and anodized
FAVOURITE RIDER:	Philippe Gilbert
FAVOURITE BICYCLE:	Keith Haring Cinelli Laser
FAVOURITE OBJECT:	A well-seasoned cast-iron skillet

FOFFA BIKES

In a tale indicative of the passion that cycling and the quest for great bikes creates, Dani Foffa began in the business in 2007 by working on vintage bicycles from his tiny flat while maintaining a career in the City of London. In 2009, he quit the day job and teamed up with photographer and fellow cyclist Tyson Sadlo to form Foffa Bikes. They opened a shop in East London, along with the help of a few passionate cyclist friends, and since then the company has launched four customizable models: Gears, Prima, Grazia and Ciao, the last a new model designed especially for urban riding.

Foffa Bikes is one of a new and growing brand of bicycle-makers who utilize both their own designed parts as well as those of other manufacturers to custom-build bicycles for their customers. Specializing in single-speed and fixed-gear bikes, the company offers two services to those who want to build their 'ultimate bike': Mix Your Fix enables clients to choose everything from frame to patterns and accessories; and Stick Your Fix allows frame customization in collaboration with designer Charlotte-Maëva Perret.

But even if all of this choice hasn't swayed potential buyers, Foffa offers a bicycle-hire scheme with a difference: if a customer loves his or her hired bike and decides to buy it, the hire cost is refunded against the price of the bike. This is bicycle business for the twenty-first-century urban market.

ESTABLISHED:	2009
LOCATION:	London, UK
BIKE TYPE MADE:	Single-speed, fixie, geared racing, geared touring, ladies' classic steel, Foffa Ciao (concept commuter)
SPECIALITIES:	'All bikes are fully customizable using online bike builders; conceptual design to offer upright posture on a lightweight commuter bike, the Ciao'
FAVOURITE RIDER:	Still riding, Chris Hoy; history-maker, Eddy Merckx
FAVOURITE BICYCLE:	'Schindelhauer designs stand out'
FAVOURITE OBJECT:	The Hövding invisible helmet

FOFFA BIKES ∞ UK

FRANCES CYCLES

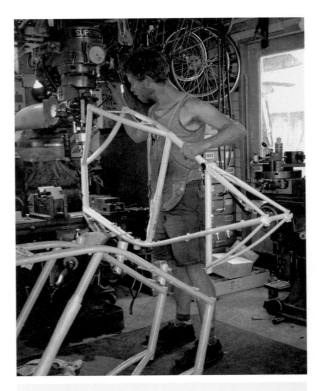

So often today bicycles are seen as high-tech racing machines or fashion accessories, but Joshua Muir of Frances Cycles aims to set the record straight about the importance of the bike in today's society. 'Bicycles offer a way to move around in the world, without sacrificing the beauty and safety of our neighbourhoods or the quality of our air,' he says. 'They are an argument for localism, and my building process reflects these ideals as best as possible. I don't own a car and drive little, riding frames out to the painter in Watsonville. Most of the materials I use are sourced within the US, and some in the Bay Area. My frame sets are built by hand, one at a time, slowly.'

But Joshua doesn't forego style in his quest to encourage others to be more mindful of their carbon footprint. His designs are offered in a number of styles – classic road bikes, randonneurs, fixed-gears in track or street set-up, mixtes and cargo bikes, both big and small – and all frames are steel-brazed, with or without lugs. Joshua custom-builds each bicycle to the client's measurements and specifications, and enjoys taking on all types of challenges. Recently, one such challenge was the Mixtehaul, a mixte-inspired cargo bike for Oregon Manifest, which can be adapted to carry babies – strapped into a baby carrier, of course – or more conventional cargo.

'I design and build beautiful, functional bicycles that best fit the end use,' Joshua says, 'while maintaining a commitment to elegant design and artistry.'

ESTABLISHED:	2006
LOCATION:	Santa Cruz, California, USA
BIKE TYPE MADE:	Cargo, road and touring frame sets
SPECIALITIES:	Modern innovations on the Long John cargo bike, introducing cable steering and new geometries; the Mixtehaul and Smallhaul
FAVOURITE RIDER:	Quentin Lindh
FAVOURITE BICYCLE:	'Every great bicycle is made great by use (I am avoiding the question) – there are so many great bicycles'
FAVOURITE OBJECT:	Opinel picnic knife – 'the one with the wood handle'

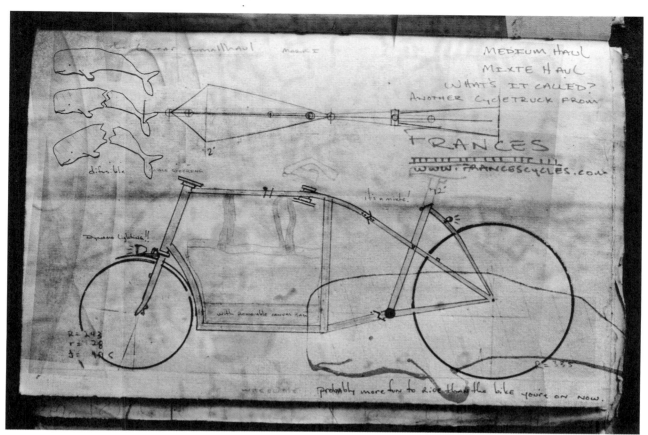

GEEKHOUSE BIKES

Self-described 'bespectacled geek' Marty Walsh founded his company Geekhouse Bikes in 2002. After working in the retail and component sector of the bicycle industry for over a decade, he apprenticed under Mike Flanigan of ANT Bicycles and learned to build his own designs. Today he uses only TIG-welding ('because it gives us the freedom to customize every joint to your specification') in making a range of bikes that includes fixed-gear models, tourers, cyclocross and mountain bikes. The frames and components are powder-coat finished, making them super-durable for all cycling types.

'Beautiful bicycles are a lot of fun to admire, but they're also more fun to ride,' Marty says. 'We work with American steel, because it's built to last. Everything we do is done with a level of intentionality that simply isn't found in off-the-shelf bikes.' He started out by designing mountain bikes, and they still hold a place in his cycling heart, but Geekhouse is now known for its cyclocross endeavours (the firm's Mudville frame is highly sought after).

The Geekhouse cyclocross team is easy to spot, owing to their bright-green and pink bikes and matching Razzle Dazzle attire for Cuppow. In fact, such is Geekhouse's notoriety on the cyclocross circuit that R.E.Load Bags have recently collaborated with the company to design a messenger bag. 'We're the dream team,' says Marty. 'We've got the best kit, and we can definitely build you your dream ride.'

ESTABLISHED:	2002
LOCATION:	Boston, Massachusetts, USA
BIKE TYPE MADE:	Handmade custom steel bicycles
SPECIALITIES:	Custom TIG-welded frames
FAVOURITE RIDER:	Dan Timmerman (Richard Sachs cyclocross team rider)
FAVOURITE BICYCLE:	'How can you choose just one?'
FAVOURITE OBJECT:	The wheel

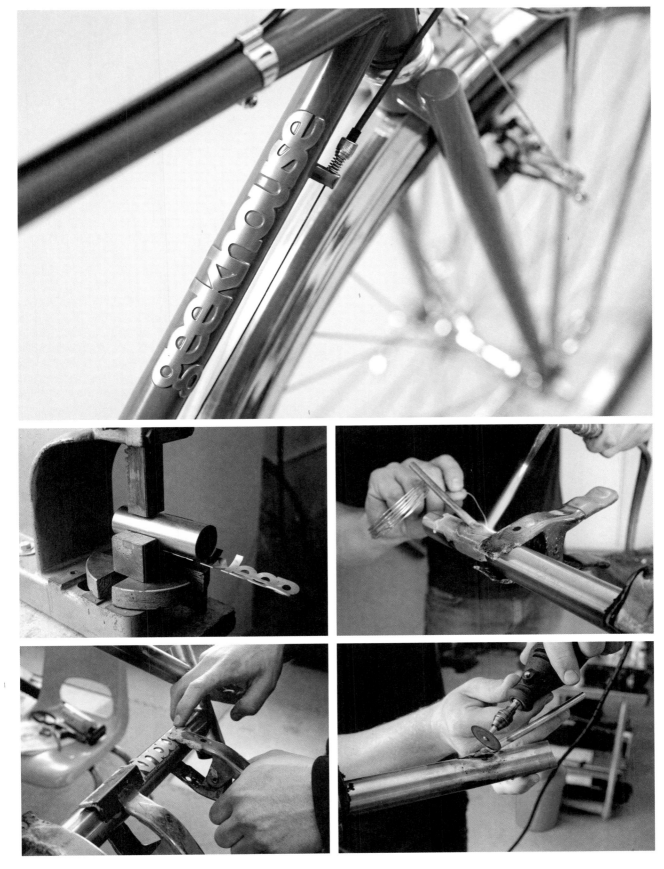

BRUCE GORDON CYCLES

Bruce Gordon, one of the most well-known custom builders in the US, is a master of his art. Bruce has been building bikes since 1974, after dropping out of graduate school at the Art Institute of Chicago and taking a frame-building class taught by Albert Eisentraut in Oakland, California. He was hooked, and decided to invest in Eisentraut's business, becoming the company's vice president. But the partnership didn't work out, and in 1976 Bruce set up his own company in Eugene, Oregon.

Since then, Bruce has built thousands of frames and bikes. Initially, his drive stemmed from the desire to use modern materials and make better bikes than those that were available from Europe at the time. 'There wasn't much coming out of Japan, Taiwan and China in those days,' says Bruce. Today, he still enjoys working in the shop. 'I love making things with forty-year-old aesthetics, but with modern materials,' he says. 'CNC machinery, computer design and old-school style – that's cool.' This fascination with new technology doesn't always extend to his material choices: 'Modern materials are harder to work with than steel on a small-shop level. I'll do it, but people are coming around to the realization that "old", meaning steel, is often better.'

When asked what he'll be doing in a decade's time, Bruce's answer is a typical one for a custom bike-builder. 'I don't make enough money to retire, so I guess I'll still be working,' he says with a wry smile. 'I really enjoy making things, so I'll probably be in the shop.'

ESTABLISHED:	1976
LOCATION:	Petaluma, California, USA
BIKE TYPE MADE:	Touring, city and racing bikes, 4130 cro-mo racks, toe clips, cantilever brakes, tail lights, panniers, titanium pumps
SPECIALITIES:	'Modern materials with old-school aesthetics'
FAVOURITE RIDER:	'Anyone who can win without drugs'
FAVOURITE BICYCLE:	'A frame made by Mark Nobilette or Peter Weigle'
FAVOURITE OBJECT:	Bauhaus designs

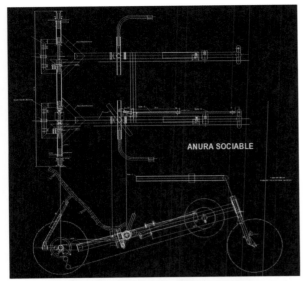

ANURA SOCIABLE

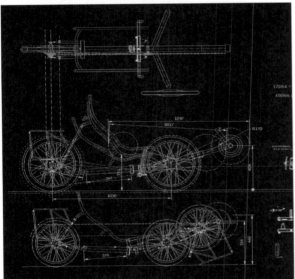

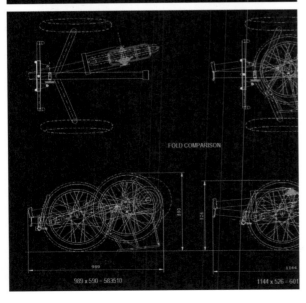

FOLD COMPARISON

989 x 590 = 583510   1144 x 526 = 601

GREENSPEED

Ian Sims is a lifelong fan of the recumbent bicycle, and of trikes in particular. Working out of Knoxfield, Australia, he started up Greenspeed in 1990, initially as a small family business, making one trike per month in the garden shed. But as the name and popularity of the designs grew, so did the business, and Greenspeed now sells as many bikes in the US as at home on the other side of the world.

A move stateside presented a new challenge – bigger bodies! 'I watched a prospective customer struggle to get in and out of my X5 model at a store in Jackson, Missouri,' Ian says, 'and I realized that this machine was no good for him, nor the many others like him.' He returned to Australia, and redesigned his trike with bigger, stronger wheels, a seat that adjusts up and down, as well as in recline. The result was a bigger, stronger X5, but the trouble was it was now quite heavy. Ian went to Taiwan and worked with aluminium engineers to create a new frame, and the Magnum was born – a trike for on- or off-road use.

Greenspeed offers quad bikes, too. Originally designed for able-bodied riders, the Anura trike picked up a new following among disabled riders, owing to its ease of mount and dismount. Its narrow wheel base made it a little unstable, however, and so Ian built the Anura Quad, a four-wheeled option that loses none of the Anura's speed or style.

ESTABLISHED:	1990
LOCATION:	Knoxfield, Victoria, Australia
BIKE TYPE MADE:	Recumbent tricycles
SPECIALITIES:	Steering geometry
FAVOURITE BICYCLE:	Velocar

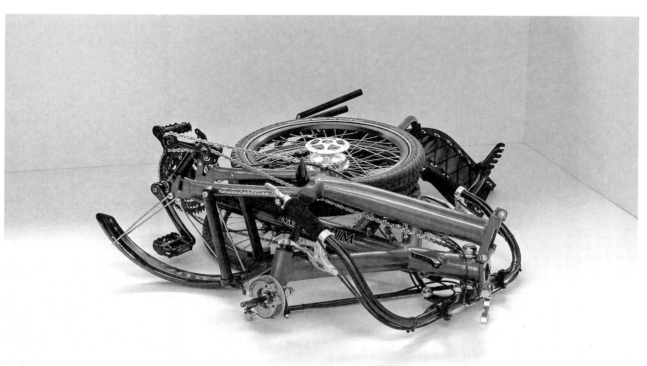

HILLBRICK BICYCLES

For a guy whose father wouldn't let him have a bike until he was twelve years old, Paul Hillbrick has certainly made up for lost time. Racing from the age of thirteen and building bikes from the age of seventeen, this Australian has now been in the business for over twenty-five years. Paul also notes that the aircraft industry, in which he served as a fifteen-year-old machinist apprentice, benefited him enormously: 'It teaches you the accuracy you need to build good frames.'

Even more of an influence was frame-builder Fred Cobcroft, who built Paul's racing frames. 'Fred said to me, "You better come in and I'll teach you properly,"' Paul recalls. 'He used a traditional forge to braze frames, and could have one completed by lunchtime.' He remembers Cobcroft as giving off the appearance of being a 'cranky, impatient old bugger', when in fact he had a heart of gold and was a great frame-builder, whom Paul came to respect hugely.

Paul later set up Hillbrick Racing, making his name with high-end custom frames. He still offers this service, along with frame repairs, a distribution base and even an indoor cycle studio, which features fitness cycles designed by Paul himself. 'Times change and you have to diversify,' he points out, but he still loves to make steel-framed bicycles. 'Classic will always come back in style – maybe not in a big way, but people appreciate the feel and longevity of a good lightweight steel frame.'

ESTABLISHED:	1988
LOCATION:	Smeaton Grange, New South Wales, Australia
BIKE TYPE MADE:	Road, track, time-trial bikes, children's racing, touring, tandems
SPECIALITIES:	'Classic; nice chrome work'
FAVOURITE RIDER:	Bernard Hinault
FAVOURITE BICYCLE:	The Italian 3
FAVOURITE OBJECT:	Classic road bike

JOSÉ HURTADO

Should concept bikes be included in this book? Some would say no, but the future begins with an idea, and so we will look forward as well as back to classic models. One such concept bike is the Twist, developed by Spanish architect-turned-designer José Hurtado. The minimalist design features single arms in place of two forks, which attach the wheels to the frame. The frame itself is a symmetrical design, and the seat and handlebars can be swivelled around a central axis to become reversed, if desired (they lock into place to prevent sideways movement when riding). A second frame can also be attached, turning the bicycle into a tandem.

'The Twist is not just a bike,' says José, 'it is a union between people.' Hubless, quick-release tyres turn the wheel rim around on its bearings; the rim is anchored to the frame at two points, thus serving as a rigid fixing point for the frame. To drive the bike forward, pedals power a chain attached to a toothed wheel, which interlocks with the teeth on the inner rim of the rear wheel. 'At first I thought the symmetrical concept could be extrapolated to accommodate any number of riders in a theoretically infinite daisy chain,' Hurtado says, 'but given the shape and attachment points of the fork, alternating frames would necessitate a third wheel, which could accommodate two forks, one on either side.'

José's design is unorthodox, but it does offer up an alternative – incorporating hubless wheels, a drive train, reversible frame and twisting mechanism – to the conventional, tried-and-tested double-diamond frame design.

ESTABLISHED:	2009
LOCATION:	Madrid, Spain
BIKE TYPE MADE:	Twist – 'a bike for a new city'
FAVOURITE RIDER:	Josef Ajram
FAVOURITE BICYCLE:	Vanmoof 3
FAVOURITE OBJECT:	Rocking chair by Charles and Ray Eames

ICARUS FRAMES

Ian Sutton is a bicycle-frame geek and he doesn't mind who knows it. Having trained under Koichi Yamaguchi at the Yamaguchi frame-building school in Rifle, Colorado, and then working as a finisher and machinist for Seven Cycles in Watertown, Massachusetts, Ian went on to design frames under his Icarus brand in order to translate his ideas into a vivid, individual reality. 'I build primarily fillet-brazed frames, which gives me the freedom to build with any tube size and shape and at any angle, but with a more polished look than welded frames,' he explains. 'I design, machine, braze and finish each frame myself, before handing over to Bryan Myers at Fresh Frame to do a world-class paint job.'

Ian works in steel because of its versatility and variety of sizes of tube, which enables him to choose tubes based on what each customer wants their bike to do. 'I don't buy sets or in bulk,' he says. 'While I primarily use True Temper tubing, which is made in the US, I can also order from elsewhere. I want to build the best for each job. With proper rust prevention, these frames can and will outlive you.' When asked why he doesn't use other materials, Ian says: 'I could argue the greatness of steel as a custom frame material against the other options that are available, but there are so many fantastic builders doing really great work with all types of materials that I thought it rude to be negative towards the non-ferrous custom frames. Choose the material that best suits you, that's what I say!'

ESTABLISHED:	2007
LOCATION:	Austin, Texas, USA
BIKE TYPE MADE:	Full custom frames of all kinds
SPECIALITIES:	Fillet-brazed construction, hand-carved details
FAVOURITE RIDER:	Marco 'Il Pirata' Pantani
FAVOURITE BICYCLE:	Yamaguchi asymmetric pursuit 1992 World Champion bike
FAVOURITE OBJECT:	The 1949 Vincent Black Shadow engine

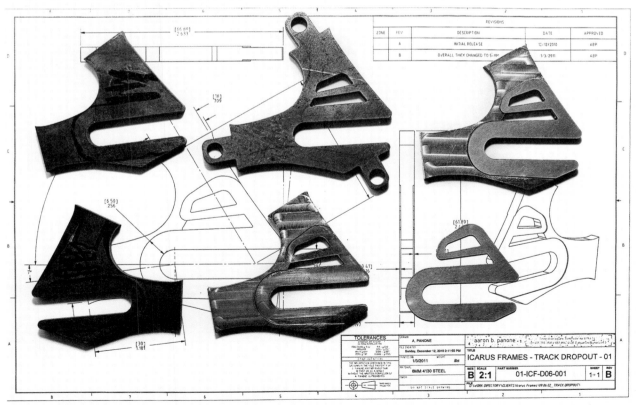

JAEGHER

Four generations of the Vaneenooghe family have built racing bicycles under the Jaegher name, beginning with Odiel Vaneenooghe in 1934. Since then, fathers and sons have passed down their art and many of the world's greatest cyclists, including no lesser a name than Eddy Merckx himself, have won the greatest races in the world on Jaegher bikes. Today, Diel Vaneenooghe and his father Luc mastermind the company, and this pair of cycle obsessives ensure that every client is correctly measured and each bike is built to the highest of standards.

Steel is their material of choice, and every custom frame is welded or brazed in the workshop in Ruiselede, Belgium. Diel is in charge of the TIG-welded frames (Ascender and Interceptor), while Luc brazes the frames with lugs (Raptor Pistier and Phantom). 'Just as the best fashion designers don't do ready-to-wear, we're not tempted by mass production,' says Luc. 'Every single Jaegher corresponds to the exact needs of its owner. In our workshop, the client is meticulously measured. It can take up to an hour to do this exactly right. Every tube of the frame is then cut and mitred exactly according to those measures. There is no such thing as "kind of right" at Jaegher.'

From Odiel to Diel, the Jaegher name remains the same, and those lucky enough to ride a bicycle made by the company understand why Merckx and his compatriots kept going back for more.

ESTABLISHED:	1934
LOCATION:	Ruiselede, Belgium
BIKE TYPE MADE:	Top-end steel bicycle frames
SPECIALITIES:	'Made-to-measure race frames built with the best steel alloys and stainless steel, both lugged and TIG-welded'
FAVOURITE RIDER:	Briek Schotte ('for his great expressions') and Jan Janssen ('for his fantastic personality')
FAVOURITE BICYCLE:	'We are continuously looking for improvements, technically and aesthetically, so our next one is our favourite'
FAVOURITE OBJECT:	Campagnolo corkscrew received as a gift from Eddy Merckx in the 1960s – 'we frequently put it to good use'

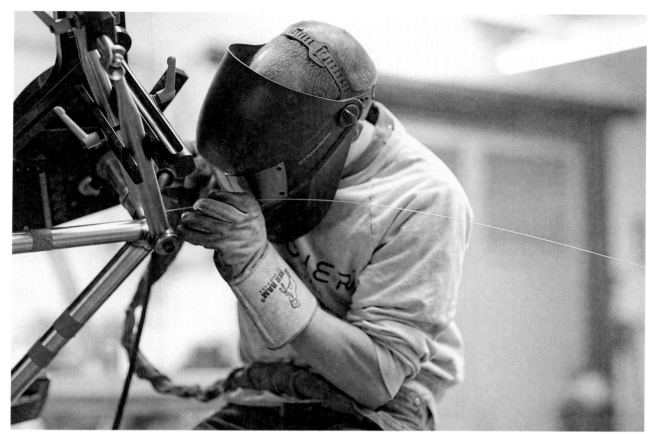

BLUEPRINT GEOMETRY
VISUAL IDENTITY
PERSONALISE WITH QUOTES
FINAL COLOUR SELECTION
PACKAGING
DELIVERY FRAME TUBES
ENGRAVE LOGO HEAD TUBE
CUT & MILL TUBES
WELD & BRAZE FRAME
CHECK FRAME ALIGNMENT
ADD ALL BRAZE-ONS
SANDBLAST FRAME
PAINT BASE-COAT
FINAL COLOUR & FINISHING
DELIVERY PARTS & PACKAGES
COMPLETE JAEGHER CYCLE
MEASURING CLIENT
JAEGHER CREW
DELIVERY OR SHIP TO CLIENT

16·07–22·07 23·07–29·07 30·07–05·08 06·08–12·08 13·08–19·08 20·08–26·08 27·08–02·09 03·09–09·09 10·09–16·09 17·09–23·09 24·09–30·09

JEFF JONES BICYCLES

Jeff Jones is a non-conventionalist, a left-field thinker, a cyclist who is committed to the non-suspended bicycle where others would be pumping up the gas and fitting extra springs. Jeff sees the mountain-bike fraternity's infatuation with high-tech suspension systems as something of a fallacy, a technological advance that goes far beyond the needs of many riders. 'Ride without the flattery of bloat-'n'-float, and less really can be more,' he says. 'It's delightful when all of your steering, pedalling and subtle weight shifts make an immediate difference to your ride.'

Jeff's designs are agile, precise, efficient, comfortable and fan-tastic fun. The Jones geometry delivers a rigid bicycle that is anything but, with frame and forks designed in harmony to deliver a pure cycling experience like no other. 'My philosophy is that if you let each part of the bike do what it needs to do to the full, without inter-ference from other parts or systems, then the bike will respond in performance,' he says. 'When parts might interfere with one another, I give priority to the one that demands priority. This is based first on safety, second on reliability, third on desired performance, and fourth, lowest weight.'

Sounds good? It must be, as Jeff has stopped taking orders for custom-builds owing to a backlog. Fortunately, his stock frames are still available.

ESTABLISHED:	2002
LOCATION:	Medford, Oregon, USA
BIKE TYPE MADE:	Frames, forks, handlebars, hubs, wheels and complete bikes
SPECIALITIES:	Rigid-specific, off-road and road, large wheels, multi-position handlebars, H-bars, truss forks and space frames – 'for function not fashion'
FAVOURITE RIDER:	'My kids'
FAVOURITE BICYCLE:	Pedersen
FAVOURITE OBJECT:	An air-cooled VW

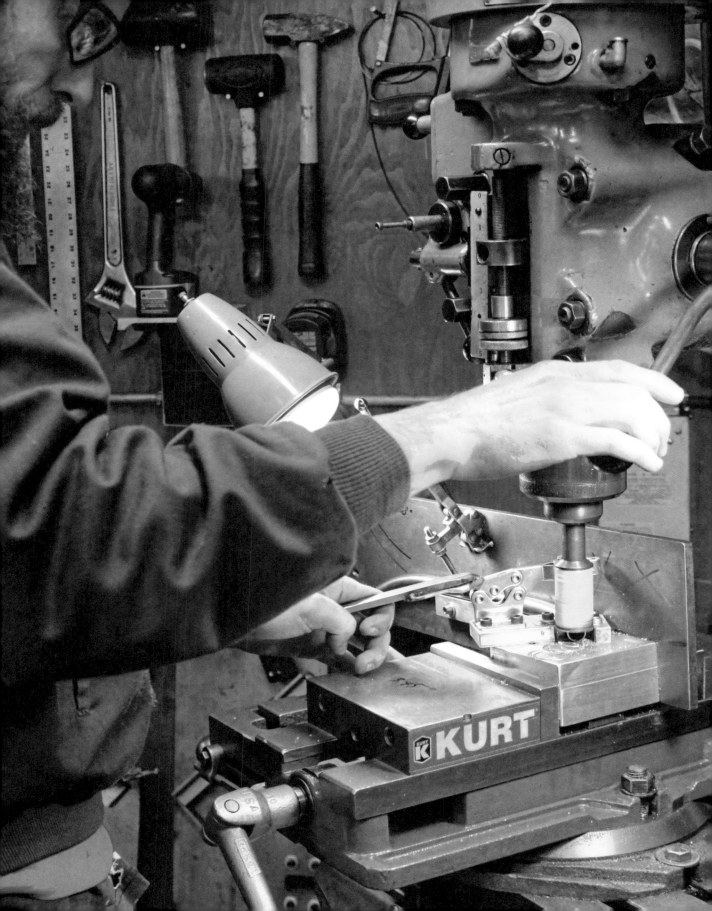

KINFOLK
BICYCLE CO

From graffiti artist to fashion designer and finally custom bicycle importer, this is the 'career' path that New Yorker Maceo Eagle has taken, ultimately leading him to working with a septuagenarian master bike-builder known only as Kusaka-san. Maceo's clothing designs were manufactured in Japan, and regular trips there put him in touch with John Beullens. The two became fanatical Keirin race enthusiasts, and soon this leisure pastime got them thinking about how people in the US might really appreciate the beautifully designed track bikes.

Maceo and John, along with business partners Ryan Carney and Salah Mason, began bringing frames back to New York, where they were snapped up immediately. Seeing that they were on to a good thing, the guys set up Kinfolk Bicycles – then came the hard part. Kinfolk wanted to offer clients a brand-new, completely hand-built custom bike in the Keirin style, but to do so, they had to find a Keirin bike-builder, which entailed many trips out of Tokyo to the small towns and villages where these craftsmen live. Eventually they met seventy-two-year-old Kusaka. 'His shop was huge, worked in,' says John. 'There was nothing out of place, and nothing there that was not necessary. As for his hands, they are hard and leathery, from a life building bicycles for the Keirin elite.'

Kinfolk now offers new Keirin bikes for sale – just five or six at a time, the maximum that can be hand-built in a month. As with many of the custom builders in this book, the waiting list is long.

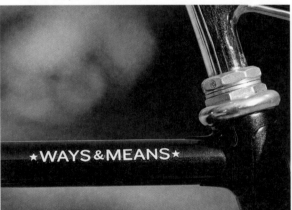

ESTABLISHED:	2008
LOCATION:	Brooklyn, New York, USA and Tokyo, Japan
BIKE TYPE MADE:	Custom frames and forks
SPECIALITIES:	Handmade bespoke bicycles from Japan
FAVOURITE RIDER:	Shawn Wolf in New York and Kusaka Yuki in Tokyo
FAVOURITE BICYCLE:	'A Tanabe-made Kalavinka is a beauty to behold'
FAVOURITE OBJECT:	Shinya Kimura custom motorcycles

KONNO CYCLE WORKS

In 1965, a year after the Tokyo Summer Olympics, Hitoshi Konno founded Cherubim with the express desire of competing on equal terms with the Italian cyclists (Mario Zanin had won gold in the Men's Individual Road Race); a mere three years later, Hitoshi was the official frame supplier for the Japanese team in the 1968 Mexico City Games. Along with his two brothers, he built up the company under the Cherubim, 3Rensho and Miyuki brands to become one of the pioneers of frame-building in Japan. Today it is run by his son, master frame-builder Shi-ichi Konno.

Konno Cycle Works continues to wow the cycling world with a combination of state-of-the-art research methods and uncompromising craftsmanship. The firm has won seven consecutive Best Bicycle Awards, and is renowned for its unusual solutions to frame design. Their Air Line bike, for example, is a study in aerodynamics (the designers believe that this kind of innovation is the only way to advance bicycle design beyond merely looking at material weight), while the Hummingbird is all about sexy. This startling frame design claimed top spot at the 2012 North American Handmade Bicycle Show for its daring lines and curvaceous appeal.

'We collaborated on the project with Simon Taylor of the UK firm Tomato,' says Shi-ichi. 'Simon provided the inspiration, and we designed this beautiful, streamlined bicycle to show the skill and ideas of Japanese makers to the world.'

ESTABLISHED:	1965
LOCATION:	Tokyo, Japan
BIKE TYPE MADE:	Road bike, track racer
SPECIALITIES:	Steel frame
FAVOURITE RIDER:	Eddy Merckx
FAVOURITE BICYCLE:	'Any bike in the golden age of steel frame'
FAVOURITE OBJECT:	'Many products and buildings from the 1960s'

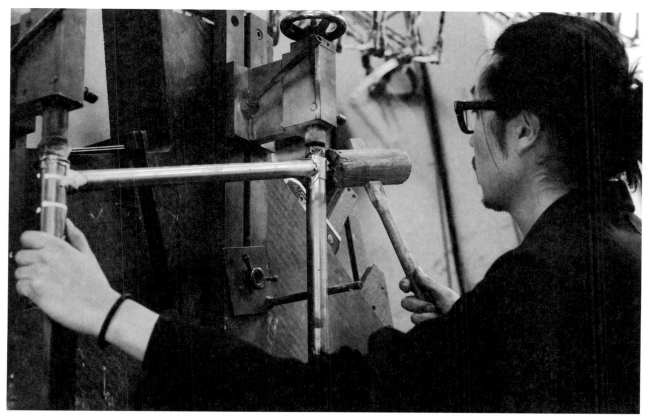

CHRIS KVALE CYCLES

'When I began in 1976, good racing frames were not always readily available, so the growing market created a demand for handmade frames,' says Chris Kvale, founder of the eponymous company and a passionate cycle racer of over twenty years. But by the 1980s newer, lighter materials, as well as mountain biking, had taken its toll on the steel-frame market and Chris found himself restoring classic steel frames. His skill at painting them also began to attract new business.

'I am essentially self-taught, and am still doing things in much the same way as I learned in my early years,' he says, 'although experience has helped me improve my skills and develop more sophisticated approaches. While others have adapted to modern times, I'm still making the same style of classic frame that I loved when I was a young racer. "Stuck in the 1970s," my wife says.'

Fortunately, there has always been a large enough market to keep Chris going. And with the current resurgence in classic and vintage bikes, his order books look likely to remain healthy. When he's not working, Chris continues to be a recreational cyclist, riding about five thousand miles a year, and taking friends on a tour each summer to Michigan's Upper Peninsula.

ESTABLISHED:	1976
LOCATION:	Minneapolis, Minnesota, USA
BIKE TYPE MADE:	Classic racing/sport frames
SPECIALITIES:	Simple, clean lines with fine filing and finishing
FAVOURITE RIDER:	Eddy Merckx
FAVOURITE BICYCLE:	Classic Cinellis
FAVOURITE OBJECT:	The bicycle – 'external, elegant, efficient, endowing its rider with grace and freedom'

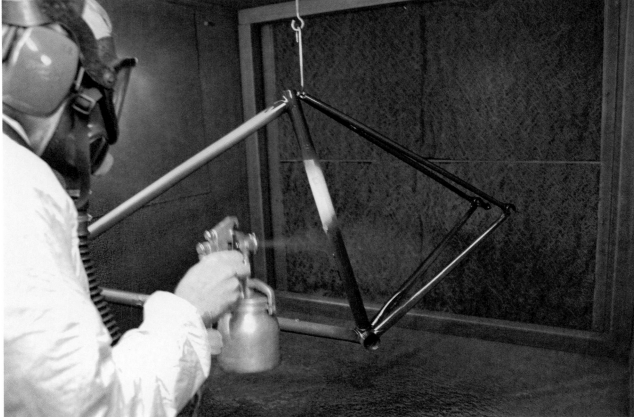

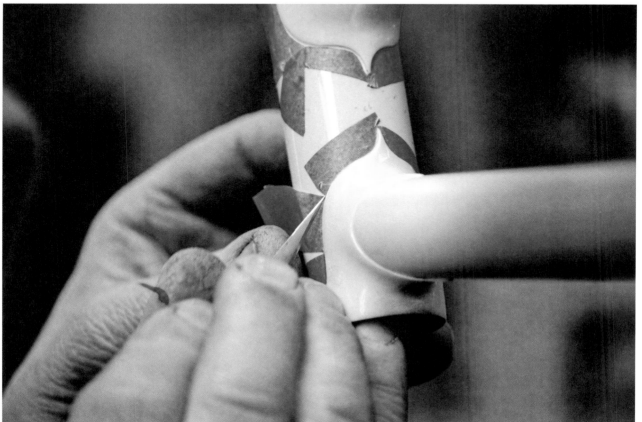

LENZ SPORT

Mountain bikes and dirt bikes have been a part of Devin Lenz's life for as long as he can remember. He has ridden since he could walk, and has read about riding ever since he could get his hands on cycling magazines. By the mid-1980s, Devin was experimenting with building his own designs, and, in 1987, he sold his first bike. Since then, the company that has become known as Lenz Sport has gone from producing eight to ten bikes a year to almost a hundred.

'I didn't do an apprenticeship or go on any frame-building courses,' says Devin. 'It was more trial and error. I read all kinds of literature, from cycling magazines to engineering books, and built what I thought would work, and would improve the riding experience. I came up with a concentric pivot design and played around with it, and kept pushing to make things better, and today I think my bikes perform pretty well.'

Devin has recently begun designing and making ski bikes, too. These frames-on-skis are still an unusual sight on the slopes, but he hopes that soon they will be picked up by the ever-expanding winter-sports market. The ski bikes are uncomplicated to build and require a less high-tech approach than mountain bikes. 'I don't like over-complication,' Devin says. 'I like the simplest of solutions – the lightest weight, simplicity of structure – and I try to embody these desires in both my mountain bikes and the new ski bikes.'

ESTABLISHED:	1996
LOCATION:	Denver, Colorado, USA
BIKE TYPE MADE:	Mountain bikes and ski bikes
SPECIALITIES:	Ski bikes and high-end performance mountain bikes
FAVOURITE RIDER:	Mike Curiak
FAVOURITE BICYCLE:	Mountain Cycle's Trek Y
FAVOURITE OBJECT:	The ski – 'not complicated, but its design is critical to its performance'

LLEWELLYN CUSTOM BICYCLES

As if being mechanic to the Australian national team wasn't enough of an introduction to the cycling world, that was once just part of Darrell McCulloch's job. When he wasn't touring, Darrell (his middle name is Llewellyn, by the way) built bicycles – for racing, touring and sports recreation. Today, after working with the national teams of twenty-three different countries (which included going to two Olympic Games and six World Championships) he still builds bikes – much to the delight of his loyal clients.

A passion for bicycles and cycling came to Darrell early, as it did for many of his peers. 'I was searching for a career path when I left school,' he says. 'Bespoke clock-making seemed interesting, but this received a negative response from the school careers advisor. While seeking my compass bearings, I was thrashing around the Brisbane streets on my Malvern Star and reading about the exploits of the recently retired Eddy Merckx. These stories inspired me on my professional path with bicycles.'

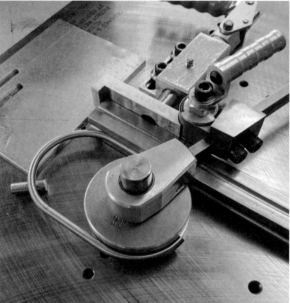

After a ten-year spell working at Hoffy Cycles in Brisbane, Darrell founded Llewellyn Custom Bicycles in 1989, all the while riding competitively in Australia and abroad. 'I gave myself a decade from when I started out in the industry to have my own marque and be building custom bicycles,' he says. 'I blend the merits of traditional lugged construction with the very best of contemporary design and materials to create functional, rationally designed bicycles with excellent aesthetics. My goal is to build clients a bicycle that will give them years of enjoyable riding. So with each passing year, their Llewellyn bicycle gives them greater value.'

ESTABLISHED:	1989
LOCATION:	Brisbane, Queensland, Australia
BIKE TYPE MADE:	Bespoke custom bicycles, road and track
SPECIALITIES:	'It's steel. It's lugs. Let the others get on with the madness.'
FAVOURITE RIDER:	'The rider in each of Frank Patterson's superb drawings'
FAVOURITE BICYCLE:	'I have yet to meet it'
FAVOURITE OBJECT:	The Supermarine Spitfire by Reginald Mitchell

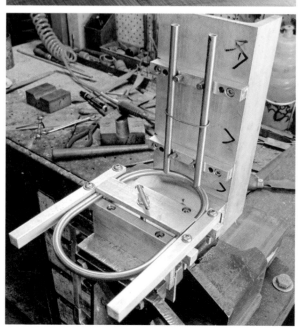

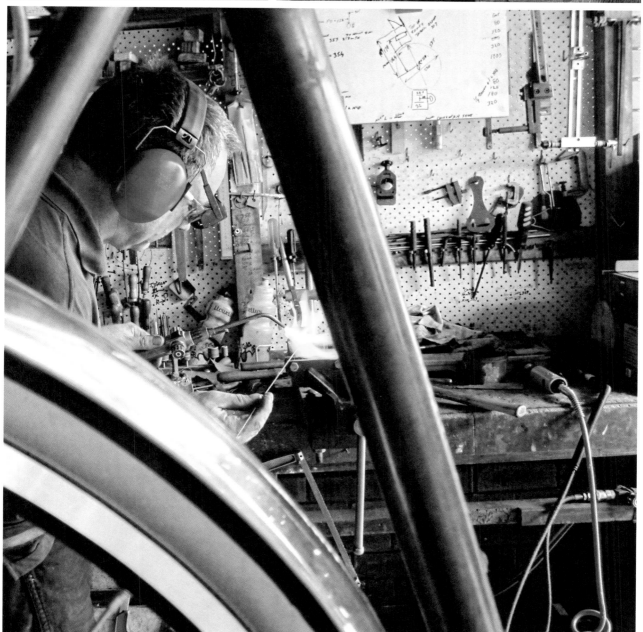

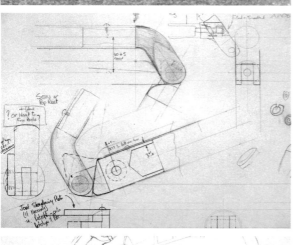

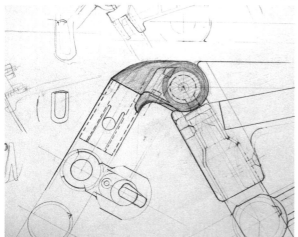

MING CYCLE INDUSTRIAL CO

When Mark Sanders embarked upon his Master's Degree project in the early 1980s, he cannot have imagined that his prototype folding bicycle would make such an impact on the urban-cycling world. Mark won the Royal College of Art's Giorgetto Giugiaro award for his work, and the bike appeared on the BBC programme *Tomorrow's World*, which in turn piqued the interest of an entrepreneur. The rest, as they say, is history.

The Strida, as the bike is now called, features a greaseless kevlar belt drive, instead of a conventional chain, to minimize the potential for getting dirty when folding the bike. When it is folded, the Strida is pushable, differentiating it from other folding bicycles that have to be carried. In terms of the design, Mark looked to the Maclaren push-chair, which has its wheels aligned to the folded form, enabling users to push, rather than carry it. 'Foldable buggies are used in just the same way as folding bicycles,' he says. 'They have to fit in car boots, on trains and buses. It made sense to take inspiration from them.'

The Strida went into production in 1986, and by 2002 some 25,000 models of Strida 1 had been sold. In 2000 production rights had moved from Roland Plastics, a UK firm, to Steedman Bass in the US; two years later, Bass moved production to the Ming Cycle Industrial Co in Taiwan to meet demand. Ming bought the rights from Bass in 2007, and continues to collaborate with Mark on refining the design to keep it ahead of the chasing pack.

ESTABLISHED:	1989
LOCATION:	Taichung, Taiwan
BIKE TYPE MADE:	Strida folding bike
SPECIALITIES:	'The triangular, belt-driven, roll-when-folded, fun folder!'
FAVOURITE RIDER:	Bradley Wiggins
FAVOURITE BICYCLE:	IF Mode – 'with Strida DNA'
FAVOURITE OBJECT:	One-touch, automatic jar opener

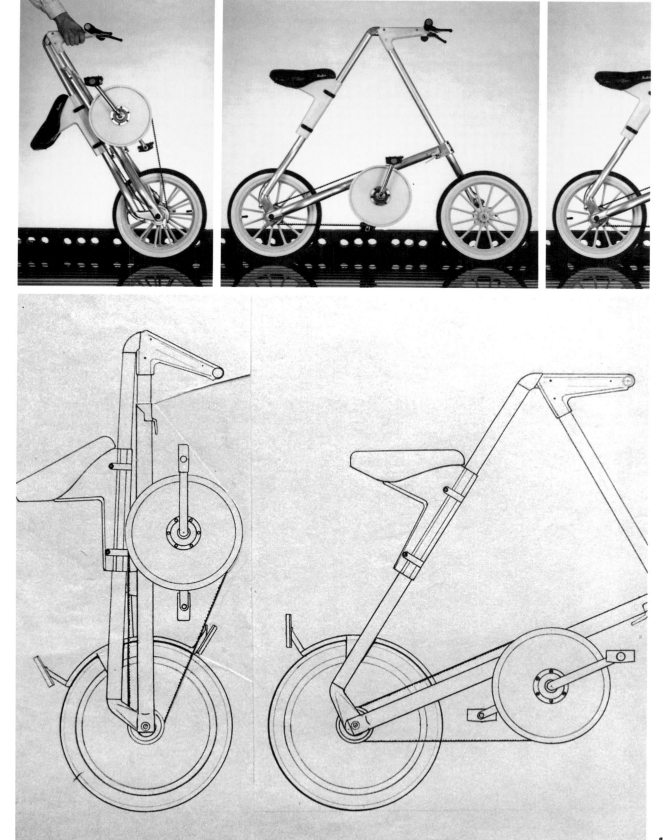

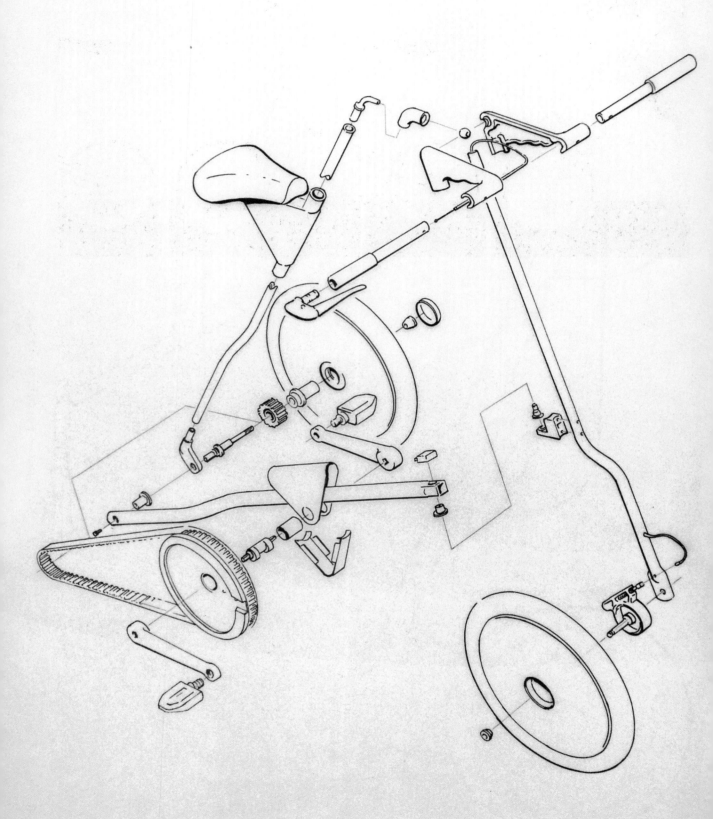

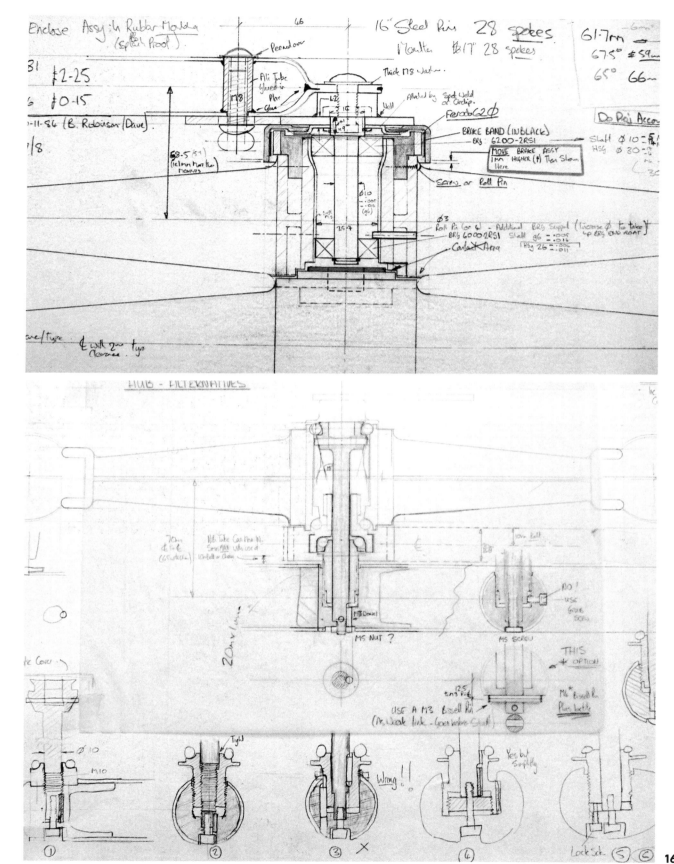

163

MISSION BICYCLE COMPANY

'Mission Bicycle Company was founded on a simple premise,' say Matt Cheney and Zack Rosen, joint owners of the San Francisco bike-maker. 'Give people the bike they want and they will ride it.' While many custom bike-builders measure up a client, just like a tailor, and then build a bike in their own style, Mission decided to do things differently. Each bike is custom-designed by its rider, with the assistance of the Mission team, who then build it by hand.

'With the help of our design staff, clients choose each bike component to best suit their riding history and expectations,' says Matt. 'We keep a menu of components in-house at all times, but are happy to reach beyond that if asked.' The firm's bikes are light, durable and made to last a lifetime. Built of cro-mo steel, the two frame designs – Valencia and Sutro – were inspired by track geometry and are intended for city commuting. As such, Mission builds both single-speed and internally geared bikes.

'We are the designers, fabricators, mechanics and retailers,' Matt adds. 'Our goal is simply to get as many people as possible the world over to choose the bicycle as transportation. To do that, we are connecting riders with bikes in a novel way by allowing them to customize not just the look, but also the riding style and utility of their bike. We are making that accessible to anyone and everyone, regardless of past cycling experience.'

ESTABLISHED:	2008
LOCATION:	San Francisco, California, USA
BIKE TYPE MADE:	Custom-built steel city bicycles
SPECIALITIES:	'Simple, durable city bikes, designed by each rider and built one at a time'
FAVOURITE RIDER:	'From bus boy to mayor, anyone who uses a bicycle for transportation'
FAVOURITE BICYCLE:	'The everyday, everywhere city bike'
FAVOURITE OBJECT:	Internally geared hubs

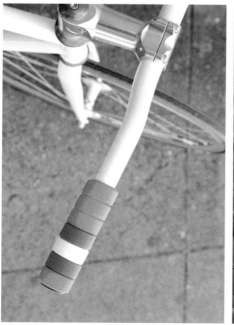

MOULTON BICYCLE COMPANY

Having celebrated its fiftieth birthday in 2012, the Moulton Bicycle Company is today the most widely recognized designer and manufacturer of folding bikes in the world. Its founder, renowned engineer and inventor Dr Alex Moulton, was still at the helm when he died during the company's anniversary year, and lived to see the firm's small-wheeled bicycle scale the heights of cycling achievement, becoming a design classic that even the most discerning commuter wouldn't want to be without.

Of the Moulton's genesis, Dr Moulton noted that the design was 'born out of my resolve to challenge and improve upon the classic bicycle, with its diamond-frame and large wheels, which has locked bicycle design into that form since the end of the nineteenth century.' His continual experimentation and improvements saw the Moulton evolve from the original F-Frame, which sits alongside mini-skirts and Austin Minis as a 1960s design classic, to the Speedsix, a racing and touring bicycle, the AM, with its distinctive space frame, and the current New Series, which features a hydrolastic suspension system.

Not content with designing a folding bicycle for the masses, Moulton also pitted his designs against racing bikes. From the outset small-wheeled Moultons broke records, beginning in 1962 with a Moulton SPEED, ridden by John Woodburn during the Cardiff–London race, covering 261km (162 miles) at an average speed of 39km (24 miles) per hour. In 1978 Daved Sanders completed the 800km (497-mile) Paris–Harrogate centenary ride in only fifty-one hours, and in 1986 Jim Glover broke his own 200m (656 ft) flying-start speed record at the International Human-Powered Speed Championships, reaching a speed of 82km (51 miles) per hour, a record that still stands today.

ESTABLISHED:	1962
LOCATION:	Bradford on Avon, Wiltshire, UK
BIKE TYPE MADE:	F-Frame, AM and New Series range of space-frame bicycles
SPECIALITIES:	'Full Moulton suspension, front and rear, using smaller wheels with high-pressure tyres'
FAVOURITE RIDER:	Dave Bogdan, in the 1988 Race Across America – 'the only rider to be able to sign his name legibly after the event'
FAVOURITE BICYCLE:	Moulton SPEED
FAVOURITE OBJECT:	Mini Classic

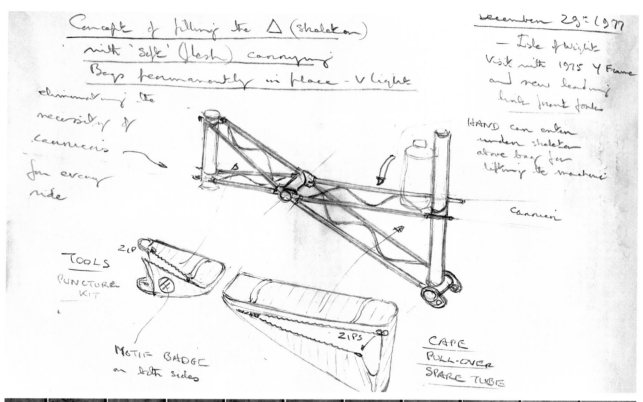

Concept of filling the △ (skeleton)
with 'safe' (flesh) carrying
Bags permanently in place – V light

eliminating the
necessity of
carriers
for every
ride

december 29ᵗʰ 1977
– Isle of Wight
Visit with 1975 Y Frame
and new leading
link front forks

HAND can enter
under skeleton
above bag for
lifting the machine

Carrier

TOOLS
PUNCTURE
KIT

ZIP

MOTIF BADGE
on both sides

ZIPS

CAPE
PULL-OVER
SPARE TUBE

NAKED

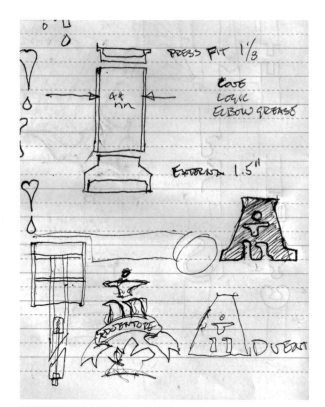

Designer Sam Whittingham has been building custom frames with 'love, logic and elbow grease' for over fourteen years. While working in bike shops he learned to weld, design, machine and paint long before he put together his first frame, and spent years racing and perfecting bike fit and riding analysis for various cycling disciplines. 'I work with bicyles and ride them everyday, and yet they never cease to amaze me,' he says. 'I love that with a few simple tools I can create something that will take someone around a velodrome in only a few seconds or around the world at just the right speed.'

Sam began racing at the age of fifteen, and has succeeded at road, recumbent and mountain-bike racing and on the track, but he is probably best known as 'that guy in the *Guinness Book of Records*, who rides a space capsule at 80mph'. His first frame, built for a friend, is still being ridden daily. Reflecting Sam and his team's love of all types of cycling disciplines, the company builds numerous kinds of bike, from track and mountain to *hors* (French for 'apart from', meaning bikes that cannot be categorized), using steel, stainless steel and titanium.

The results are award-winning bikes – securing both the top prize and People's Choice award at several North American Handmade Bicycle Shows – designed and built by bike fanatics.

ESTABLISHED:	1998
LOCATION:	Quadra Island, British Columbia, Canada
BIKE TYPE MADE:	Handmade bicycles, all types
SPECIALITIES:	'All 100 per cent fully custom, handmade bicycles. Each bicycle is unique'
FAVOURITE RIDER:	Beryl Burton
FAVOURITE BICYCLE:	Varna speedcycle by George Georgiev
FAVOURITE OBJECT:	'The bicycle, of course'

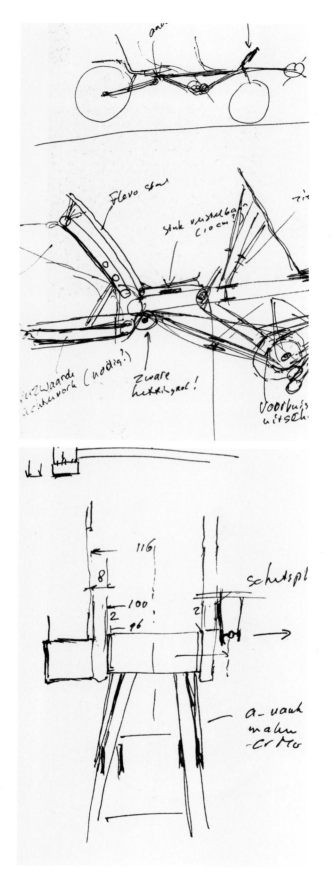

NAZCA LIGFIETSEN

In 1998, Henk van der Woerdt formed Innovative Cycle Works, a one-man business that would eventually become Nazca Ligfietsen. Initially based in Hengelo, Netherlands, Henk designed a suspended recumbent with foldable handlebars, and although he had wanted to market several different products, this first bicycle was so well received that he soon decided that recumbents were the way to go.

Eventually settling on the brand name 'Nazca' (after the pre-Inca civilization in Peru), Henk joined forces with partner Monique Holterman to launch Nazca Ligfietsen (*ligfietsen* being Dutch for 'recumbent'). Since then, the duo have expanded their operations – outsourcing production and powder-coating of the frames to fellow Dutch manufacturer Rainbow – and at last count have hand-built and sold well over 2,500 recumbent bicycles around the world. Nazca Ligfietsen now has eight models in a large number of versions to its credit. The range includes the Gaucho 28 high-racer, a model with an upright riding position and high handlebars, and the Fuego, the company's newest and most laid-back recumbent.

Henk has also recently designed and built a recumbent tandem, the Quetzal, a dual-rider model that uses the Gaucho as a basis and extends things from there. 'After the handmade prototype was tested, the design was finalized and the first Quetzal tandem built,' Henk says. 'Two days after its completion, Monique and I took it on a three-week holiday to France, cycling approximately 1,400km (870 miles), with full camping gear attached.'

ESTABLISHED:	2000
LOCATION:	Nijeveen, Netherlands
PRODUCT:	Recumbent bikes, tandem and parts
SPECIALITIES:	'Reliable, hand-built cro-mo frames, intended for loaded travelling and touring'
FAVOURITE RIDER:	Peter Haan
FAVOURITE BICYCLE:	M5 Low Racer
FAVOURITE OBJECT:	Velox 2, fully faired recumbent bike

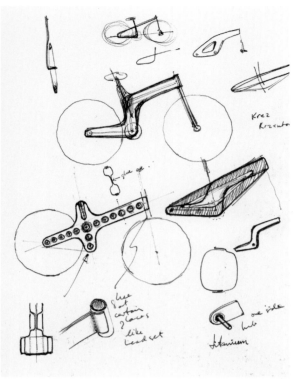

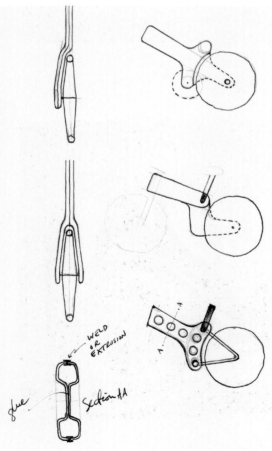

MARC NEWSON

Today a world-famous designer of everything from furniture to aircraft, in his late teens and early twenties Marc Newson was a self-proclaimed 'bike nutcase'. Obsessed with bicycles from a young age, he had always wanted to design one. 'In terms of engineering, bikes should be fairly straightforward,' he says. 'But having realized all of that, I understood that if I didn't really interject something bold and groundbreaking, it was going to be a boring bike. I wanted to make something different.'

Marc had seen a technology called super-forming in action, and he could see its potential. The process, in which aluminium is vacuum-formed, enables almost any shape to be realized. 'On a bicycle frame, it's like joining the dots,' he says. 'I took all the most important parts and joined them with the fewest lines. It's all about reduction, which implies that the bike wasn't going to be made from tubular metal joined together.'

Aluminium is the material of choice, both for super-forming and for many other bicycle designs, owing to its strength-to-weight ratio and cost-effectiveness. The frame for Marc's MN01 bicycle for Danish firm Biomega had to be made in two halves, which were bonded together (rather than welding) for ease and speed, and to avoid reheating the metal. The basic frame is the same in all the designs Marc produced for Biomega. The first four models were made from aluminium, but the latest incarnation features an ultra-lightweight, carbon-fibre frame. The MN03, a single-gear, bi-disc town bike, was chosen by the Centre Georges Pompidou in Paris as one of the ten most innovative products at the turn of the millennium.

ESTABLISHED:	1997
LOCATION:	London, UK
BIKE TYPE MADE:	Biomega
SPECIALITIES:	'Frames of super-formed aluminium, bonded together with an epoxy resin linking front forks and handlebar to the seat, with the lower bar of the Z-frame securing the rear wheels'
FAVOURITE RIDER:	Felice Gimondi
FAVOURITE BICYCLE:	Cinelli Laser Nostra
FAVOURITE OBJECT:	Concorde's nose cone

NOBILETTE CYCLES

Mark Nobilette has been interested in bicycles and cycling ever since his high-school days. 'I became very interested in high-end bicycles back then,' he recalls, 'mostly because I had discovered Campagnolo components, which led to an overall appreciation of bicycles and riding.' Mark also had a friend who was experienced in metalwork, and when he heard about a frame-building course taught by Albert Eisentraut, he just had to be in the class: 'I was the last one to get a place, but I was the only one offered a job afterwards. I accepted it immediately, and moved to California to begin what has since been my life's work.'

Mark worked with Eisentraut for a year and a half, before setting up on his own and founding Nobilette Cycles in Ann Arbor, Michigan, in 1977. His work has changed in the forty years or so he has been building frames – and influences have shifted from Italian build-ers such as Faliero Masi, Cino Cinelli and the like to the French con-structeurs, including René Herse, Alex Singer and Jo Routens – but he still prefers to build in steel. 'The biggest advancement in frame technology is the heat treating of steel tubing, allowing it to become lighter and stronger,' says Mark. 'There are obviously new materials for frames that have become common since I've been building, but apart from being lighter in weight, I don't believe that the new mater-ials have made better frames.'

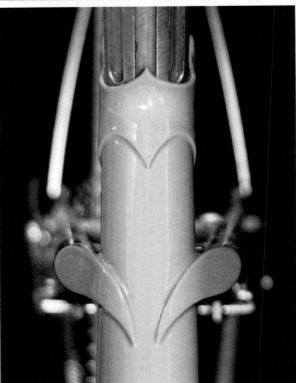

ESTABLISHED:	1977
LOCATION:	Longmont, Colorado, USA
BIKE TYPE MADE:	Road, randonneur, cyclocross
SPECIALITIES:	Exquisite finishing and unusual frame styles
FAVOURITE BICYCLE:	Albert Eisentraut designs, as well as those of René Herse and the French constructeurs

NORWID

Founded in 1992, Norwid is the brainchild of Rudolf Pallesen, an avid fan of bicycle touring. Like many other custom frame-builders, Rudolf began his career by working in a bike shop, before apprenticing in 1988 at Hans Lutz's bicycle works in Blaubeuren, southern Germany. He branched out on his own just four years later.

Rudolf builds around 150 custom frames each year, offering a variety of models, all based around the touring style. He believes that the current resurgence in custom-made bicycles is due to a variety of reasons, from environmental issues to a backlash against the global economic troubles. 'Some of our customers are conscious of the environment and of their health, some are tired of all the cheap imports and want to create their own style,' Rudolf says. 'Others prefer to get something for their money before the banks squander it.'

Rudolf's passion for touring led to his owning a Koga Miyata frame back in the early 1980s, a style of frame that remains his inspiration. 'Now I try to combine the good features of steel with modern engineering – oversizing to stiff up the frames – and classic design,' he explains. But he freely admits that the most important advances in the cycling industry are the high-end carbon-fibre and e-bikes: 'Even though they hold no interest for me, I think carbon frames and e-bikes are the most important news,' he says. 'Nevertheless, I will continue to produce classic steel bikes.'

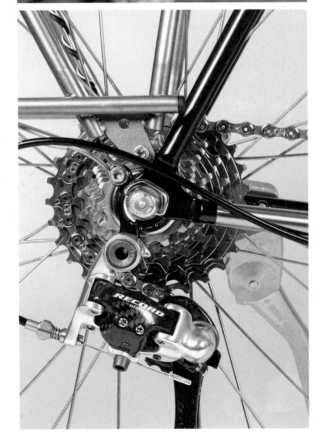

ESTABLISHED:	1992
LOCATION:	Neuendorf bei Elmshorn, Germany
BIKE TYPE MADE:	Tourers, randonneurs, racing bikes, mountain bikes (cyclocross/marathon)
SPECIALITIES:	A lot of stainless steel, Rohloff, randonneur
FAVOURITE BICYCLE:	Norwid Skagen

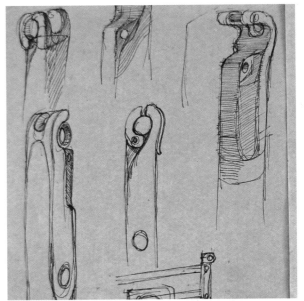

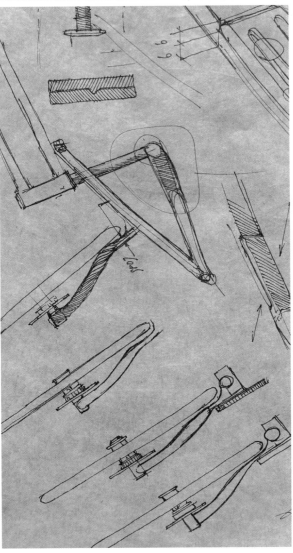

MIKULÁŠ NOVOTNÝ

Folder is the name of a folding bicycle by Czech designer Mikuláš Novotný, created while he was studying industrial design at the Academy of Arts, Architecture and Design in Prague. Mikuláš does not, in fact, specialize in bicycle design – his work encompasses architecture and product design, such as a flexible flashlight and a coffee maker. This lack of immersion in the cycling industry, however, has enabled Mikuláš to look at the challenge of folding bicycles with fresh eyes. Unlike other folding bikes, his design has full-size wheels, enabling it to be rolled along when folded.

'Folder is a folding city bicycle with 26-in. [66 cm] wheels,' says Mikuláš. 'Its greatest advantage is that it keeps its mobility, even after folding. Within a minute, it can be transformed into a compact wheelbarrow, which you can take with you on the Underground, the bus, tram, lift, wherever you want, rolling it along.' The folding system is based on the rotation of the rear wheel and forks around the seat post, and the front fork around its shoulder. Finally, both wheel hubs are joined and fixed by a central plug. There are three quick-releases that can be opened and closed.

'During the design process, I concentrated on the simplicity and reliability of the final product,' Mikuláš says. 'The frame of the proto-type is made from chromium-molybdenum thin-wall tubes, which are cheap, long-lasting and easily repaired. As for brakes, there is a two-disc brake system. In addition, it's possible to lock up Folder by pulling a lock through both the wheels and the frame.'

ESTABLISHED:	2011
LOCATION:	Prague, Czech Republic
BIKE TYPE MADE:	Folding city bicycle
SPECIALITIES:	Folding bike with full-sized wheels

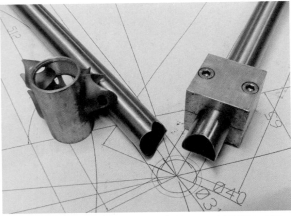

PAULUS QUIROS

'A signature feature of our bike is the hand-crafted stainless-steel plate between the seat stays and the top tube,' says Jonathan Paulus, co-founder of bicycle-maker Paulus Quiros, based in South Wales. 'A number of names were suggested for it, including Mosquito and Dragonfly. We liked Dragonfly because of the Welsh connection, and it gives us great pride that people admire our elegant solutions to this junction of tubes.'

This attention to detail is something that Jonathan and frame-builder José Quiros have taken great care to maintain since building their very first bike. 'With this level of meticulous bike construction, working to the tightest of tolerances, we can never produce a high turnover,' continues Jonathan, 'but we find there is great satisfaction in producing the very best bike we can.' Inspired by José's Catalan heritage, the firm's bicycles have a curvy beauty that makes them stand out from the crowd. Add to this the fact that Paulus Quiros is located near to Wales's velodrome, which dates to the turn of the twentieth century, and the company's roots in inspirational cycling history become clear. It is no surprise, therefore, that Paulus Quiros has only one material of choice: steel.

'Since the origin of the bicycle, steel has been bent, shaped, forged, brazed and welded to offer an immense heritage of design that no other material can match,' Jonathan says. 'There are huge advantages to using steel over other materials, and modern steels enable you to decide the final feel and behaviour of your bicycle. We believe steel provides us with the maximum degree of flexibility for our bike designs.'

ESTABLISHED:	2009
LOCATION:	Burry Port, Carmarthenshire, UK
BIKE TYPE MADE:	Bicycle frames, stems, racks, pedal cages, and more
SPECIALITIES:	'Understated elegant solutions to design and engineering problems, plus our own design of cable bosses'
FAVOURITE RIDER:	[Jonathan] Nicole Cooke and disabled riders [José] Miguel Indurain
FAVOURITE BICYCLE:	[Jonathan] BSA curved-tube folding bike [José] Cinelli Laser from 1980
FAVOURITE OBJECT:	[Jonathan] Engineer/inventor Sir Frank Whittle [José] Jaguar E-Type, the DeLorean and Rolex

PEGORETTI CICLI

Pegoretti bicycles are easy to spot, and are almost always a surprise. Clients ordering a Pegoretti model can even, if they wish (or dare), order a Ciavete paint scheme and leave the decoration entirely in founder Dario Pegoretti's supremely capable hands. 'If you order a Ciavete,' says the firm's marketing manager, 'you will get a frame hand-painted by Dario, but the colours and graphics will be whatever he chooses to do at the time, ensuring that each bike is one of a kind. Don't ask for a copy of a paint scheme you have seen before, as the idea behind Ciavete is that each frame is a unique work of art, showcasing Dario's creativity.'

After training with Italian master bike-builder Gino Milani, Dario set up his own workshop and began building frames under his own name. He was among the first European frame-builders to embrace lugless TIG-welding to build premium bicycles, and has worked with such cutting-edge manufacturers as Excel and Dedacciai in the development of new materials and tube sets. Currently, Dario builds only a few bicycles by hand each year. His bikes and their extravagant paint designs are cherished as much for their artistic merit as for their smooth ride.

ESTABLISHED:	1991
LOCATION:	Caldonazzo, Italy
BIKE TYPE MADE:	Road frames
SPECIALITIES:	Custom steel frames and one-of-a-kind paint schemes
FAVOURITE RIDER:	Eddy Merckx
FAVOURITE BICYCLE:	Dave Kirk, Mark DiNucci, Richard Sachs, Llewellyn
FAVOURITE OBJECT:	Chairs

PETOV DESIGN

Industrial and graphic designer Peter Varga hadn't even thought about designing a bicycle until 2004, when a friend suggested he enter the International Bicycle Design Competition, taking place in Taiwan that year. Despite being new to bicycle-making, his Klapeto design was chosen among the top twenty finalists. Peter has since participated another four times, making the top twenty three times. Upon graduating from the Academy of Fine Arts in Bratislava, he chose to design another bicycle for his graduation thesis: the result was Fajnyje2, a foldable city bike. 'I was inspired by the work of several designers, including Ross Lovegrove, Dieter Rams and Konstantin Grcic,' he says, 'and bikes like the IF Mode, Strida and Brompton, along with many other less well-known design studies and prototypes that I came across during my research.'

The unusually named Fajnyje2 looks like other folding bicycles, but its extremely simple, quick-folding mechanism has made it an award-winner. The unique four-point pivot design enables users to fold the bike in as little as three seconds – perfect for a hectic city commute and hopping on and off buses and trains. 'People like bikes like this because they are efficient, but also unusual,' Peter explains. 'They want to ride something that appeals to their imagination and is a little different from other mainstream models. I am still new to the bicycle-design world, but I see many custom bike designs: some are prototypes, some are limited-edition hand-built bikes. Either way, people enjoy them.'

ESTABLISHED:	2005
LOCATION:	Gelnica, Slovakia
BIKE TYPE MADE:	Prototype
SPECIALITIES:	Folding city bicycle – 'folds in just two to three seconds, stands on its wheels'
FAVOURITE BICYCLE:	Strida, IF Mode
FAVOURITE OBJECT:	Nature

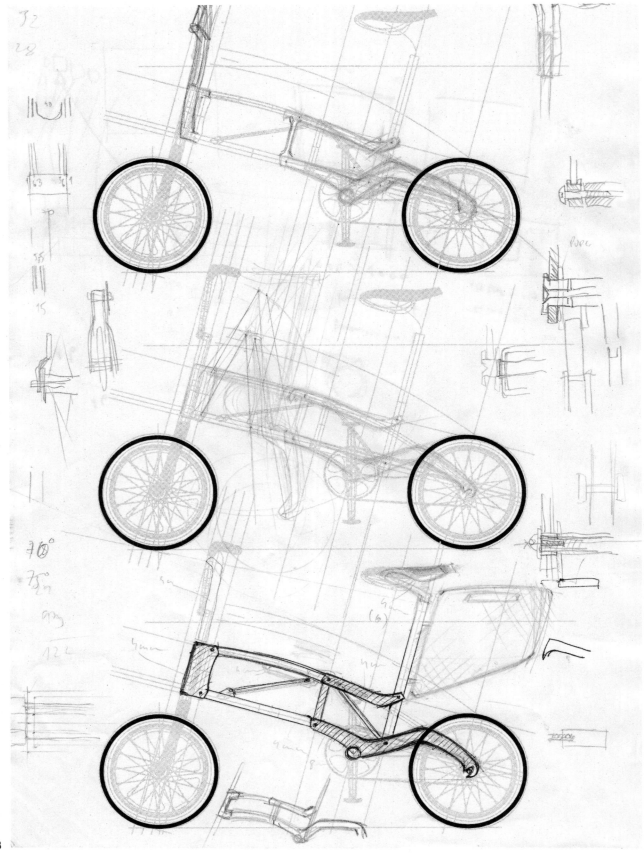

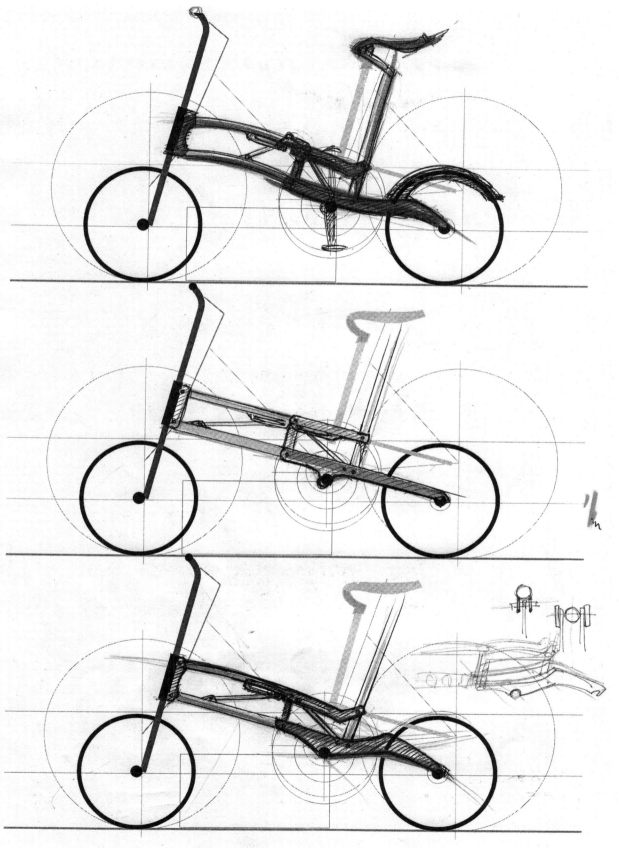

PONY BIKES

The majority of makers in this book hand-build bicycles, which are custom-fitted to their clients' requirements. There are those, however, who simply can't afford a bespoke bicycle. Where should they go for their riding pleasure? A good place to start is Pony Bikes in Melbourne, Australia. While the company doesn't build frames for the general public (yet), it does do just about everything else when it comes to pedal power. If you want a frame repaired or modified, new parts fabricated for an out-of-production classic or simply the coolest paint job on the block, Pony is the go-to jack-of-all-trades.

The team specializes in taking an old, broken bike and turning it back into a gleaming stunner, from BMX, racing, city and tourer bikes to kids' tricycles. They also offer a variety of finishing options: powder-coating, chroming, anodizing, the list goes on. 'The reality is that we can do pretty much anything you can think of,' says the team. This is not high-end custom bike-building, but the results coming out of the Pony workshop would fool many into thinking you had spent that kind of cash. The lesson learned is that 'old and tired' does not always mean ready for the bin. Look again at that rusty bike in your garage and wonder just what you, or Pony, could make of it.

ESTABLISHED:	2009
LOCATION:	Melbourne, Victoria, Australia
BIKE TYPE MADE:	Custom to any specification
SPECIALITIES:	Custom, modifications, restoration and repair work, fabrication
FAVOURITE RIDER:	Anyone with two wheels
FAVOURITE BICYCLE:	Monkey Likes Shiny gravity bike
FAVOURITE OBJECT:	Myford lathe

PRIMATE FRAMES

Extreme-sports enthusiast Tarn Mott likes to jump off cliffs with a parachute strapped to his back and kite-surf the big waves of the Southern Hemisphere. He is also a mountain-bike junkie, and hard riding is what got him involved in building bicycles in the first place. 'I was making my own rigs and modifying things I wasn't happy with when I met John Bodzefski of Cycle Underground,' he says. 'I commissioned him to build my dream bike at the time, a DH-rig based on a Brooklyn Machine Works race link. One thing led to another, and I became completely immersed in the design. John convinced me to have a go at building a bike myself, and, once bitten, there was no turning back.'

That was in 2002. Tarn worked with Bodzefski for another two years, and eventually established his own marque, Primate Frames, in 2005. Tarn currently builds ten to twelve bikes per year, revelling in coming up with unique and original designs. 'My main aim is to create bicycles with beautiful clean lines, which have a real tactile feel to them,' he says. 'It has taken me many years doing a lot of different things to find what it is that I really love doing, and to acquire the skills base to do it well. If I can continue to grow and learn in this industry, then I'll be happy for years to come.'

ESTABLISHED:	2004
LOCATION:	Balgownie, New South Wales, Australia
BIKE TYPE MADE:	Touring, fixed, road, tandem, folding, BMX, street, suspension, cyclocross, 29er
SPECIALITIES:	'Unique and original designs, bespoke designed and produced fittings and components'
FAVOURITE RIDER:	'Everyday guys who hit the road with no set destination or time frame, and end up riding halfway round the planet'
FAVOURITE BICYCLE:	Brooklyn Machine Works race-link frame, Risse Racing Lassen and Curtis Thumpercross
FAVOURITE OBJECT:	'The coffee roaster I built myself, but my anvil jig would be a close second'

PRIMATE FRAMES ∞ AUSTRALIA

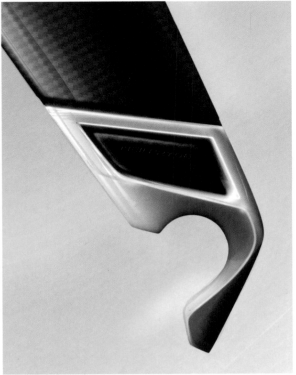

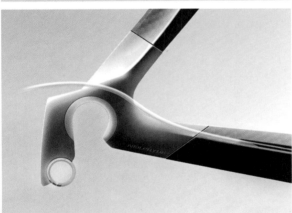

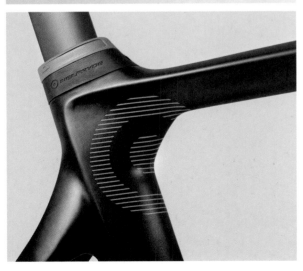

NEIL PRYDE BIKES

Neil Pryde Bikes is the culmination of one man's passion for cycling and drive to produce world-class racing bikes. Mike Pryde, the son of company founder Neil Pryde, now heads up the business, which is renowned for its marine-sports gear, including windsurfing and kite-surfing rigs. Being a cyclist at heart, however, Mike made use of the company's already considerable expertise in carbon-fibre design and manufacture to develop a range of bicycles that are good enough to be used by professionals.

'The jump to cycling was a natural progression for the Pryde Group,' Mike says. 'As a competitive cyclist with many years of racing behind me, I was passionate about developing bikes that could perform at pro level, as well as being relevant to weekend warriors aspiring to climb the most demanding alpine passes or beat their personal best times on their regular training ride.'

Mike's immense enthusiasm for the project was combined with years of design and engineering experience gained by working on cutting-edge architectural projects for the likes of Foster + Partners. Taking full advantage of Neil Pryde Bikes' know-how in composites and aerodynamics, he worked in collaboration with BMWGroup DesignworksUSA to ensure that their bike designs optimized the stiffness-to-weight ratio and that drag forces were reduced to a minimum. 'All this means is that whether you're a pro looking to take milliseconds out of your opponents, or a keen amateur aiming to burn your mates on training rides,' says Mike, 'you have the advantage.'

ESTABLISHED:	1970
LOCATION:	Hong Kong, China
BIKE TYPE MADE:	Road, time trial and triathlon
SPECIALITIES:	Wind-tunnel tested bicycles, designed using CFD with BMWGroup DesignworksUSA
FAVOURITE RIDER:	Jake Keough, Rory Sutherland and Boy van Poppel
FAVOURITE BICYCLE:	Neil Pryde BURAsl
FAVOURITE OBJECT:	Hong Kong International Airport

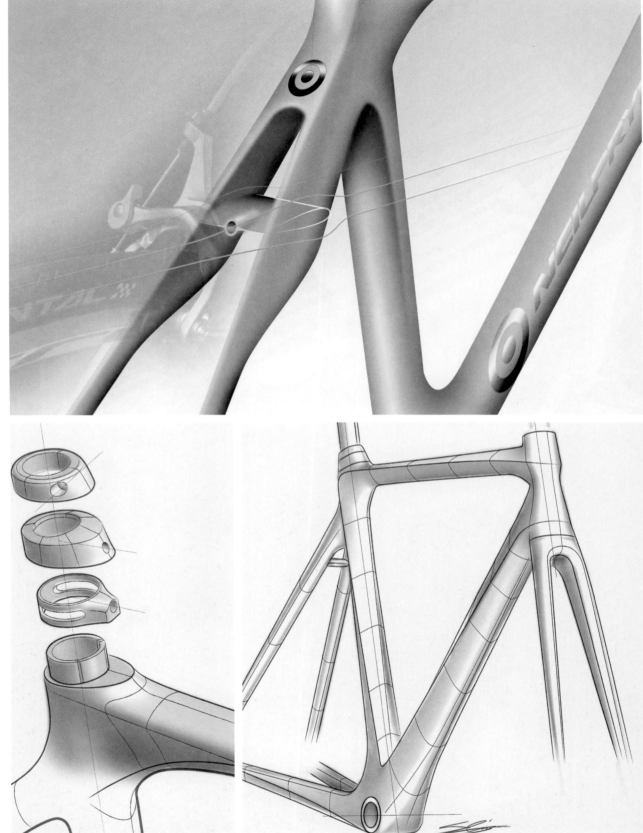

torsion

stiffness

torsion

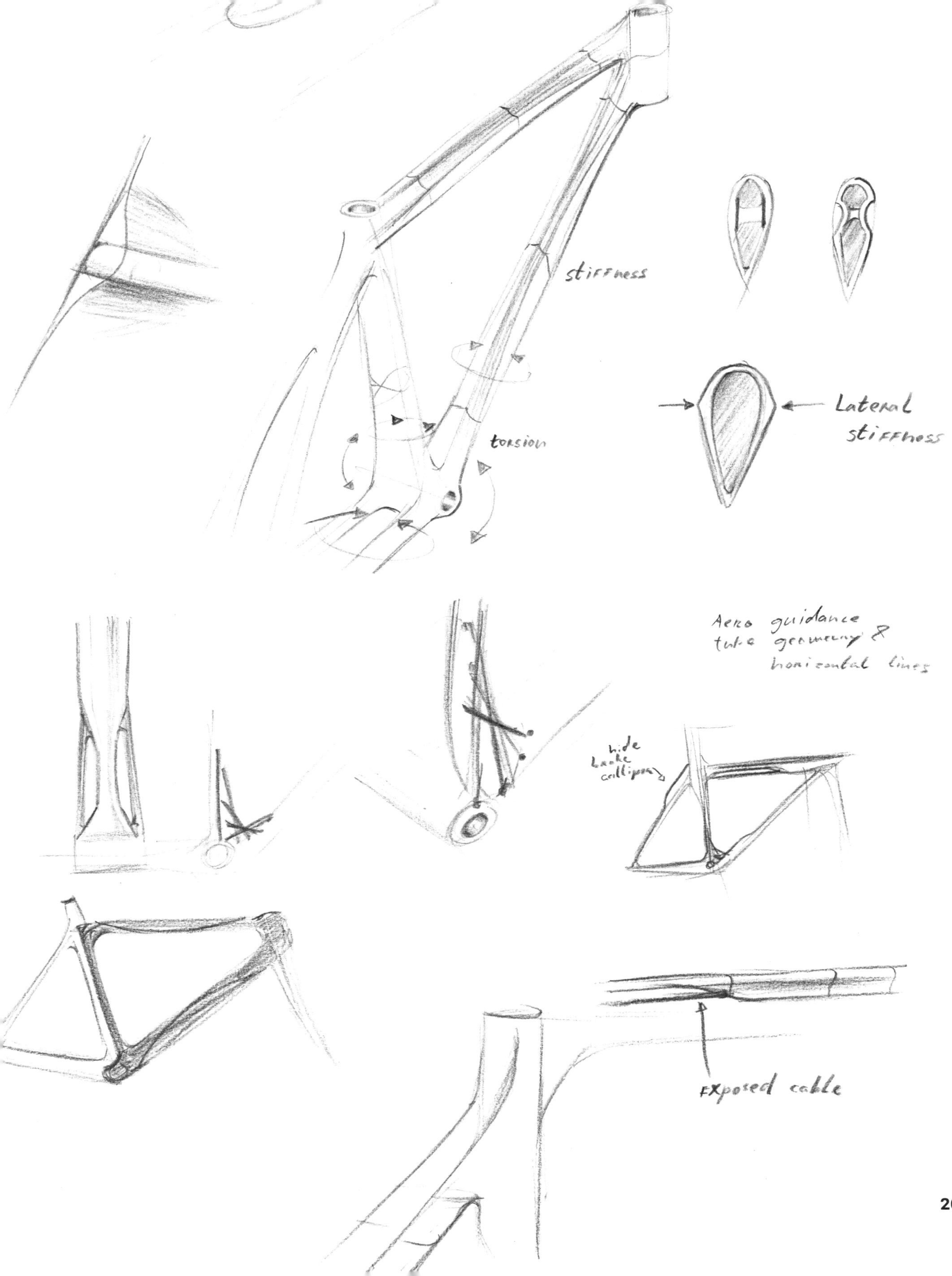

stiffness

torsion

Lateral stiffness

Aero guidance tube geometry & horizontal lines

hide brake callipers

EXposed cable

201

RETROVELO

'Yesterday is today, and today is tomorrow,' say Matthias Mehlert and Frank Patitz of Retrovelo. 'For us, "retro" means a return to the true values, those not represented by the ever-present retro-hype.' They go on to explain that although their bikes might not necessarily have mass appeal, they are aimed at a niche market that prizes quality and beauty.

'We are continuing a long tradition of locally based craftsmen, proposing an alternative future in times of industrial mass production,' say Matthias and Frank. At their manufacturing plant in Leipzig, Germany, the team has worked hard to develop a bike that is infused with tradition, while incorporating the best in contemporary design. An example of this ethos is their triple-plated crown fork, which was designed to accommodate a 70mm (2 ¼ in.) tyre. The designers soon realized, however, that they would have to design the tyre, too. Enter the Fat Frank balloon tyre, developed exclusively in collaboration with Schwalbe for Retrovelo.

These fat tyres are a feature of both the Classic Series and the new Modern Series, which lean towards a cross between BMX and mountain bikes. In all cases, the team tout the bikes' comfort and practicality, owing to their robust design. 'The uniqueness of a Retrovelo design is due to the large amount of in-house development we put into it,' says Frank. 'We build each bicycle from scratch to a harmonious whole: bicycles for riders who value authentic originals.'

ESTABLISHED:	2003
LOCATION:	Leipzig, Germany
BIKE TYPE MADE:	'Savestylish-comforturban'
SPECIALITIES:	Balloon Racer cro-mo and women's frames; triple-plated crown fork with internal cable housing; Fat Frank balloon tyre
FAVOURITE RIDER:	Arne Thomae of Ponyvelo
FAVOURITE BICYCLE:	'Joe Breeze's original Schwinn klunker'
FAVOURITE OBJECT:	Fat Frank tyre

ROCK LOBSTER CYCLES

Based in Santa Cruz, California, Paul Sadoff is a household name in custom bike-building circles, and frames from his Rock Lobster brand are highly sought after. He built his first frame in 1978 while working as a bike mechanic, and kept doing it as a hobby for another decade. By this time word had got round, and Paul was inundated with requests for frames. 'The onslaught of telephone frame orders made it necessary for me to quit my job and build frames full time,' he says. The year was 1988, and since then Paul's designs have been ridden at the Olympic Games, and at World Championship cyclo-cross and mountain-bike events across the globe.

Rock Lobster frames are built using a variety of materials and methods. While most frames are TIG-welded, fillet-brazing and lugged construction are also available for most steel frames. Paul's inspiration was born out of necessity, but each frame he has made has helped him to refine his craft. 'Now that I have been trying to redeem myself for over twenty years,' he says, 'the bikes have got to new heights of quality.'

Paul sees the industry today as coming of age in many ways. 'For a time there were a few posers and pretenders,' he says, 'but in the last ten years a group of sincere and dedicated people have come up from trade schools and apprenticeships. This new crop of frame-builders are elevating and adding sincerity to a craft that has needed it for a long time.'

ESTABLISHED:	1988
LOCATION:	Santa Cruz, California, USA
BIKE TYPE MADE:	Frames, forks and stems, complete bicycles
SPECIALITIES:	Cyclocross, single-speeds of all types, road-racing frames, track frames
FAVOURITE RIDER:	'Major' Taylor
FAVOURITE BICYCLE:	Bruce Gordon road
FAVOURITE OBJECT:	Doge's Palace, Venice

ROCK LOBSTER CYCLES ∞ USA

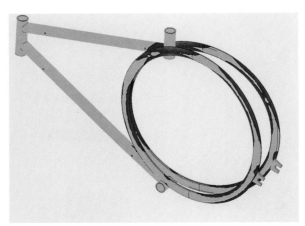

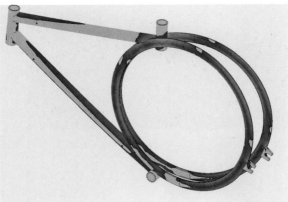

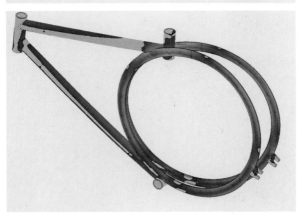

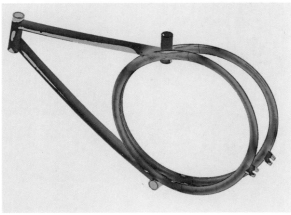

ROUNDTAIL

With a few exceptions, bicycles typically have a diamond-shaped frame, and they have done so since the early twentieth century. So why change? Avid amateur cyclist and entrepreneur Lou Tortola had an achy back caused from riding hundreds of miles on one such diamond-framed bike, and it got him thinking: why not change the frame design to make it more comfortable?

'With conventional frame geometry, the jarring vibrations from bumpy roads travel straight up the rear forks to the seat and rider's spine,' Lou says. 'Bicycle companies have spent millions on developing composites to reduce impact and increase shock absorption, but what they haven't changed is the frame shape. I saw this as the answer.' Lou's own design does away with the seat tube and stay, and replaces them with two circular tubes: 'I deduced that they would better absorb the bumps without compromising performance or lateral stiffness.'

Lou built his prototype in collaboration with Montana-based frame-builder Paul Taylor, and four months after the initial contact with Taylor the first RoundTail bicycle was delivered. The design was launched at the San Diego Custom Bicycle Show in 2011, and it immediately set the frame-building world alight. 'People are amazed and intrigued,' Lou says. 'They love it.' He has been quick off the mark, too: there are now five RoundTail models, ranging from a mountain bike to hybrids and the newest road-racer, Diamante.

'Years ago, the diamond-frame was the way to go because of limitations in manufacturing ability,' Lou says. 'That may have been the case in the 1900s, but today we can do almost anything. We can radically alter the design of a bike frame to produce a better, more comfortable ride for everyone.'

ESTABLISHED:	2011
LOCATION:	Windsor, Ontario, Canada
BIKE TYPE MADE:	Aluminium, carbon-fibre, titanium, steel
SPECIALITIES:	'Unlike the typical bike design, we use two rings to support the weight of the rider'
FAVOURITE RIDER:	Marco 'Il Pirata' Pantani
FAVOURITE BICYCLE:	The RoundTail bike
FAVOURITE OBJECT:	The CN Tower in Toronto

RUNOUT INDUSTRIES

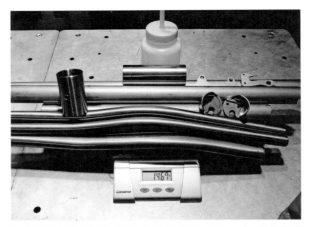

Chris Read sees a common thread between ice climbing and cycling. While the link might not seem immediately obvious, he points out that both disciplines require commitment and self-motivation, qualities that Chris, as the owner and frame-builder at Runout Industries, has put into his relatively new company.

'My career over the last ten years as a mechanical designer has introduced me to several hands-on skills, from machining and welding to fixture design and metalworking,' he says. 'This exposure produced another passion altogether: working with my hands and making things. So in 2008, I attended the United Bicycle Institute's titanium frame-building course and built my first handmade frame.'

Two years later, Chris founded Runout Industries in Canmore, Alberta, at the foot of the Canadian Rockies. The company is in an ideal location, not only for cycling and mountain biking, but also for the manufacture of its high-performance bicycles. 'The area provides a great riding atmosphere, access to materials, tooling and the most talented hands in manufacturing that Canada has to offer,' Chris notes. He and his team now build road, mountain, touring, cyclocross and all manner of bicycle frames.

'Our mission at Runout Industries is to build and deliver the best-quality custom bicycles for our clients,' Chris says. 'If you are looking for a true one-of-a-kind bike, built just for you, we can help you achieve your dream.'

ESTABLISHED:	2010
LOCATION:	Canmore, Alberta, Canada
BIKE TYPE MADE:	Road, cyclocross, track and time trial, commute and mountain bikes
SPECIALITIES:	Titanium
FAVOURITE RIDER:	Eddy Merckx
FAVOURITE BICYCLE:	The fixed-gear or single-speed
FAVOURITE OBJECT:	The blackboard

SAFFRON FRAMEWORKS

Matthew Sowter chose to follow his dream of becoming a frame-builder in 2009, and he hasn't looked back. The opening of Saffron Frameworks from a small workshop in Camberwell, South London has been a triumph. 'I didn't come from a fabrication background,' he says, 'but my love of bicycles and cycling meant that I knew what a good bicycle was and I understood how it should feel.'

Matthew trained as a welder, and worked for a time at Enigma Bikes (pp. 98–9) – 'sharpening my skills and learning more about the trade' – but all the while, the dream was to set up his own frame-making business. At Saffron, Matthew builds a small number of frames each year with the help of his team, all of whom have backgrounds in racing bikes on and off-road. 'We may not be the oldest established company,' he says, 'but we have a true understanding of how a bike should handle and perform. That's important to us.'

Today, Matthew says his love of bikes and cycling continues to grow, whether building or riding them. 'The experience I've gained has given me an ideal base from which to create and express my own interpretation of the craft,' he says, 'something I now do every day. I really enjoy turning every client's dream into a tangible reality.'

ESTABLISHED:	2012
LOCATION:	Camberwell, London, UK
BIKE TYPE MADE:	Road racing, cross-country, cyclocross, jump, town, commuter, track, touring
SPECIALITIES:	'Each frame starts with a blank canvas and evolves into a functional form as the relationship develops with the customer'
FAVOURITE RIDER:	Burry Stander – 'a quality rider and a true gentleman'
FAVOURITE BICYCLE:	The Rover (1888) – 'the first bicycle to hold the record for accomplishing twenty-one miles in an hour'
FAVOURITE OBJECT:	Copper pot stills

SANITOV

Cargo bikes are becoming a passion among a growing number of bicycle builders: they combine the alfresco experience of cycling with the load-carrying capability of a much bigger vehicle. And none does this more successfully than the CB ('cargo bike') by Danish company Sanitov. 'Our mission is to provide mobility to the urban dweller at low cost, for the health, the heart and the environment,' says designer Alexander Høst.

The CB is the product of the cultural meeting of traditional Chinese bicycle design and a functionalistic Danish approach. It is a humble cargo bike, but one infused with the latest technological know-how and Scandinavian minimalism. 'Sanitov produce intelligent and sustainable solutions to urban living and movement,' Alexander explains. 'We aim to make the urban everyday experience easier and more sustainable by creating innovative design solutions that might, in turn, shape the future city.'

The CB's design includes matching full-leather handles and saddle, high-quality stainless-steel and aluminium frames and rack, an innovative GPS tracker system and a battery-driven engine. The company's ideals are not the same as conventional bicycle-makers – it doesn't strive for the perfect speed machine, for example – but it does push the cycling ideal in the same way that many more traditional makers would approve of.

ESTABLISHED:	2009
LOCATION:	Denmark
BIKE TYPE MADE:	The Sanitov CB e-trike and single-speed
SPECIALITIES:	Scandinavian minimalism, high-quality spec and functionality
FAVOURITE RIDER:	'Because we design bicycles for urban transportation and joy, we don't have a favourite rider'
FAVOURITE BICYCLE:	The general Dutch bike look from the 1930s and '40s, Peugeot's skinny Dutch bike frames from the 1970s
FAVOURITE OBJECT:	Marcel Breuer's Wassily chair or Anish Kapoor's *Cloud Gate* in Chicago

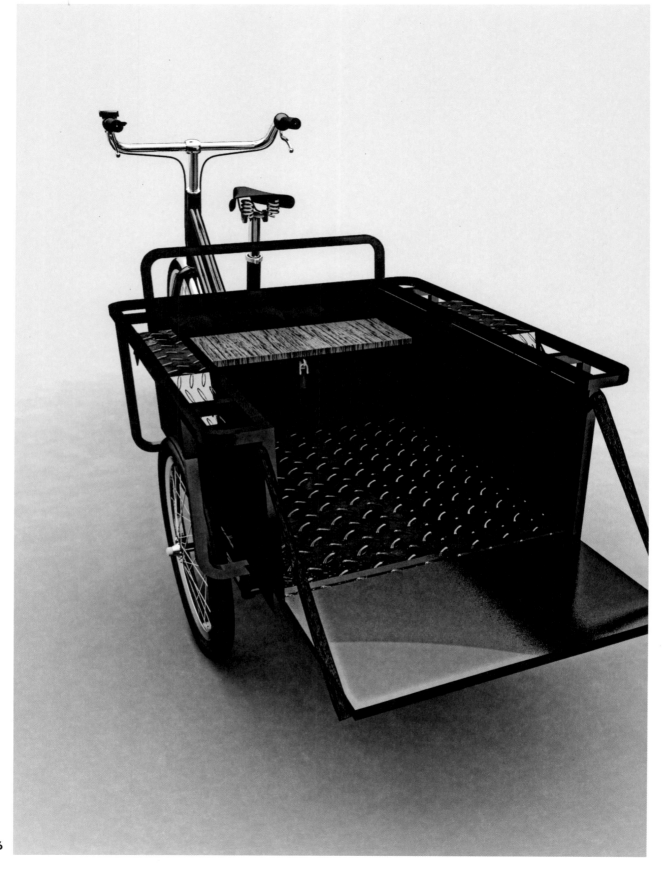

SANOMAGIC

Japanese craftsman Sueshiro Sano, a ninth-generation shipwright, has been handcrafting boats, furniture and other beautiful products fashioned out of wood for years. So his decision in 2008 to design and build a bicycle almost entirely from wood was, while unusual, not altogether unimaginable. Sueshiro chose mahogany as his base component, citing its flexibility and stress-responsiveness, which is superior to metal. 'Using mahogany lends a certain feel that a metal frame cannot,' he says, 'which in turn gives riders an elevated sense of control and increases pacing possibilities.'

To prove his point, Sueshiro has raced a number of his designs professionally, with the wooden bikes turning in times that are on a par with their metal and carbon-fibre competitors. Not content with competing, he is on a continuous quest to refine his design for a mahogany bicycle. In the eleven bikes that he has built so far, Sueshiro has managed to reduce the overall weight from 11 kg (24 lbs) down to around 8 kg (18 lbs). To further reduce the bike's weight and improve aerodynamics, he has also modified the seat-set design, replacing the metal rails and joints with mahogany ones and creating a fully integrated seat post.

'Combining the seat post and tube into one piece, running from the bottom bracket to the seat, does eliminate adjustability,' says Sueshiro, 'but it also offers the opportunity for the rider to have a completely tailored fit. I am always trying to make the best bike I can for the rider.'

ESTABLISHED:	2008
LOCATION:	Tokyo, Japan
BIKE TYPE MADE:	Wooden bicycles and ships
SPECIALITIES:	Wooden track and road bicycle

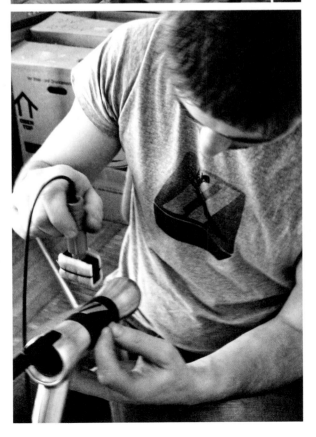

SCHINDELHAUER BIKES

Ludwig, Siegfried, Viktor and Lotte are not the names of the company's employees, but of the bicycles themselves. These quirky monikers are the first hint that the bikes made by the German firm are not your standard urban rides. Schindelhauer is a relative newcomer, set up in 2009 by four ambitious young entrepreneurs. The quartet came to the market with a pared-down street bike, with stylish looks matched by state-of-the-art technology, including a toothed belt drive rather than a chain.

This street bike, Ludwig XIV, is the flagship – or 'flagbike' – of the Schindelhauer range. It combines the new Gates' CenterTrack belt drive with the efficiency of a fourteen-speed Rohloff Speedhub. The company's own patented Belt Port II technology, along with the slider-belt tensioning system on the dropout, bring the combination with the toothed belt into balance. Even fully equipped with hydraulic disk brakes, Ludwig XIV is lightweight, weighing in at just 11.9 kg (26 lbs), thanks to the aero-shaped tubes and triple-butted, Rohloff/Gates-compatible aluminium frame. The integrated seat clamp and smoothed welding, along with Brooks leather appliqués, add to Schindelhauer's individual style.

'When we look back on the last few years, we are surprised and proud,' says co-founder Jörg Schindelhauer. 'Surprised, because we never expected to be this successful, and proud because of the amount of hard work that is paying off now. It is great for us to see our products bringing joy to people. That is the greatest reward.'

ESTABLISHED:	2009
LOCATION:	Berlin, Germany
BIKE TYPE MADE:	Urban bicycles
SPECIALITIES:	Belt-drive bicycles
FAVOURITE RIDER:	Danny MacAskill
FAVOURITE BICYCLE:	UBC Coren
FAVOURITE OBJECT:	The new Aston Martin Vanquish

227

SHAND CYCLES

Formed in 2003 by Steven Shand, this bicycle company is intent on bringing cycle manufacture back to Scotland. Steven and his partner Russell Stout, proud Scots both, note: 'Scotland has a long heritage of bicycle-building, and both of us look forward to seeing "made in Scotland" appearing once again on high-performance production bicycle frames.'

Steven has been involved in the cycling and outdoor industry for over twenty years, working with some of the biggest brands. Despite this, he's still passionate about riding, and for the cost of a pint will tell you about his sponsored debut on the mountain-bike race scene way back in 1991. Russell got into mountain biking and road cycling after an addiction to fell and endurance ultra-running. He was fit enough and crazy enough to compete in triathlons in the mid-1990s, but, as he puts it, 'common sense prevailed after realizing that Neoprene and I don't agree.'

Together, Steven and Russell build production frames for road, all-road and cyclocross bikes. 'Although described as "production frames", in reality each of these is built by hand alongside our custom frames,' Steven says. 'Tubes are fillet-brazed, rather than TIG-welded, which takes longer but results in beautifully smooth, seamless joints.' As for custom builds, Steven explains that the production frames probably give a good idea of the type of bikes that the company build, 'but if you're looking for something a little bit different, we can start from a blank piece of paper and work with you to create a frame design that will fit you perfectly.'

ESTABLISHED:	2003
LOCATION:	Livingston, West Lothian, UK
BIKE TYPE MADE:	Full bikes and frames
SPECIALITIES:	Simplicity, and a liking for go-anywhere, drop-bar bikes
FAVOURITE RIDER:	John Tomac
FAVOURITE BICYCLE:	'Too many to mention!'
FAVOURITE OBJECT:	The Forth Rail Bridge

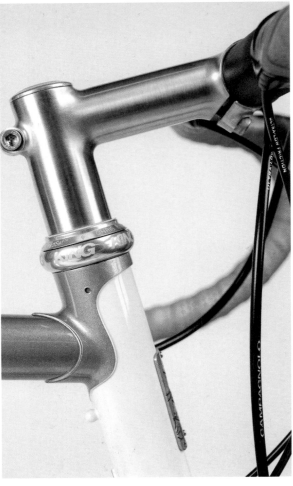

SIGNAL CYCLES

Building beautiful bikes does not have to mean big production facilities. In fact, the opposite is often the case. Take Oregon-based Signal Cycles, for example, founded by Nate Meschke and Matt Cardinal in 2007 after discovering their mutual love of cycling and making.

'We realized that we had followed a similar path,' says Nate. 'As young boys, we had loved riding our bikes and drawing. We both went on to find jobs working in bike shops, and, after a few too many years of turning wrenches, decided that art school was a good idea. We each graduated with degrees in Fine Art (Painting), and realized we were perfectly equipped for working in a bike shop.'

Paint brushes and welding torches are not common bedfellows, but Signal Cycles, which specializes in handmade bikes, was born from the creative fire that burns in this bike-mad duo. 'We love using our hands and brains to build beautiful machines that get raced on, or ridden to exotic places. Bicycles are in our blood,' says Matt.

The pair recognize the joy that people experience when working with a custom builder and being able to collaborate, discuss, design and shake hands with the people who make their bikes. 'There is a lot of talk of a new golden age of handmade bikes, and the US builders are leading the way,' says Nate. 'We're proud to be part of this custom-built renaissance. We wouldn't want it any other way.'

ESTABLISHED:	2007
LOCATION:	Portland, Oregon, USA
BIKE TYPE MADE:	Lugged and fillet-brazed steel bikes, road, cyclocross, touring, city, mountain
SPECIALITIES:	Colour palette and attention to detail
FAVOURITE RIDER:	'Any kid learning to ride without training wheels – the "pros" have been ruining the sport for too long'
FAVOURITE BICYCLE:	A used one
FAVOURITE OBJECT:	American-made vices

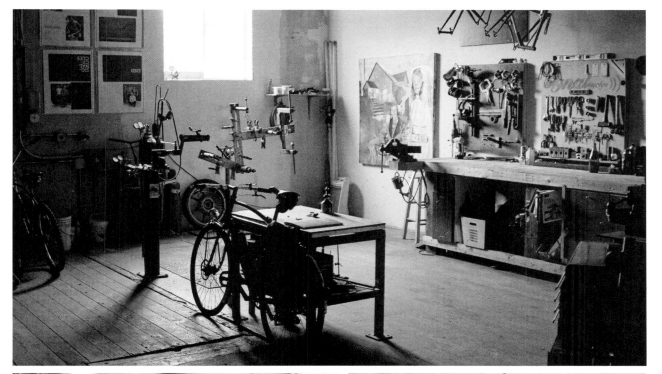

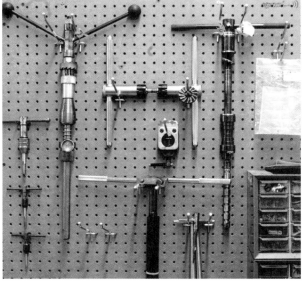

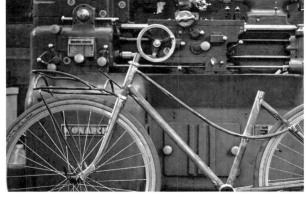

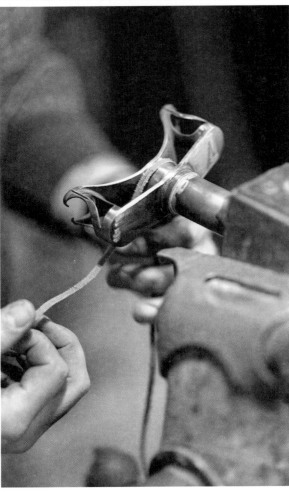

SIX-ELEVEN BICYCLE CO

'Bicycles have been enormously important to me from a young age, much more so than other childhood toys,' says Aaron Dykstra, founder of Six-Eleven Bicycle Co. 'I grew up hearing my grand-parents tell stories about the time they spent touring Europe by bicycle after World War II. My grandfather would paint a romantic picture of the terrain and the quaint little villages they visited. Though my grandparents are gone, those stories continue to motivate me.'

Like many bike-mad kids, Aaron began racing in his teens and got a job at a local bike shop. Serious cycling took a back seat when he joined the Air Force, and it wasn't until he came back from post-9/11 deployment in the desert that he could pursue his dream of building bicycles. Moving first to New York and then to Chicago, Aaron eventually wound up living back in his hometown of Roanoke, Virginia. After studying frame-building under master-builder Koichi Yamaguchi, he spent the next year honing his skills with the torch.

Today, some five years later, the company produces a range of track, tourer and road bikes, combining performance and design to create the ultimate in lugged and fillet-brazed custom steel bicycles. And the name? It was chosen, Aaron says, because 'it evokes the ingenuity and craftsmanship that made the legendary Great 611 steam engine.' Now who's painting romantic pictures?

ESTABLISHED:	2008
LOCATION:	Roanoke, Virginia, USA
BIKE TYPE MADE:	Custom steel bicycles, built for nearly every discipline
SPECIALITIES:	'Timeless bicycles that are classic yet modern'
FAVOURITE RIDER:	Fausto Coppi – 'although Greg LeMond, Sean Kelly, Graeme Obree, Nelson Vails and Ned Overend are all up there as well'
FAVOURITE BICYCLE:	Any of Francesco Moser's Hour-era bikes
FAVOURITE OBJECT:	J-class steam locomotives, built by Norfolk Southern in Roanoke, 1941–50

SMAN CRUISERS

The year was 2001, Arnolt van der Sman was fifteen years old, and he had just made a decision that would dictate the course of his life and lead to the creation of some of the most unique bicycles around today. 'I wanted to work with my hands,' he remembers, 'instead of just getting my high-school diploma and working behind a desk.' So he enrolled at the Hout en Meubilerings (Wood and Furniture) College in Amsterdam on a course that would teach him traditional woodcraft and furniture-making skills.

Many would have gone on to be a carpenter or cabinet-maker, but during his first year at college, Arnolt read a newspaper article about Vinicio Magni, the famed Italian maker of wooden bikes. 'The article captivated me, and it never let go,' he says. 'For my final examination project, I made a 24-in. [61 cm] beach-cruiser bike. I tried to make as much in wood as possible – the fork and the handlebar – but there was no time to make wooden rims.'

Arnolt designed that first bicycle in 2004, and graduated a year later with the seed of a design for a stretched cruiser already in his head. 'You learn more on every project,' he says, 'whether you're building a chair, closet or bike. Many designs later, I came up with the crossed swing-arm for the cruiser. That was in 2009.' Since then, Arnolt has expanded his range and continues to build wooden bikes using his favourite materials: ash and beech.

ESTABLISHED:	2011
LOCATION:	Hoorn, Netherlands
BIKE TYPE MADE:	Cruisers
SPECIALITIES:	Solid wood frames, no metals or composites inside
FAVOURITE RIDER:	None
FAVOURITE BICYCLE:	Van Hulsteijn – 'I'd love to do one in wood'
FAVOURITE OBJECT:	'Designing a track bike for a friend – he wants to compete in a triathlon on a woodie'

SPECTRUM CYCLES

Tom Kellogg's name resonates throughout the bicycle-making industry. Anyone who's anyone in cycling knows Tom Kellogg. This wasn't always the case, of course – even this bike-building guru was an apprentice once ... well, sort of: 'I graduated from the University of Rochester in 1976 with a BA in Sociology, and signed on for a five-year apprenticeship with custom frame-builder Bill Boston, of Swedesboro, New Jersey,' Tom recalls. 'I was fired about two-and-a-half months later!'

This minor setback didn't deter him, however, and after building frames in his shed for a year, Tom founded Tom Kellogg Frames. Within three years, the company's bikes had been ridden to two professional World Championships, two amateur silver medals and over twenty national championships. When he set up Spectrum Cycles in 1982, housed in a 185-year-old stone barn in the heart of the Lehigh Valley in eastern Pennsylvania, Tom's goal was to produce the highest-quality custom steel and titanium frames and bicycles in the world. Three years later, frame-builder and long-time friend Jeff Duser joined the team.

Custom steel frames are available for road, track, touring and cyclocross: 'Sorry, but we don't do mountain bikes,' says Tom. Each frame is designed and built by Tom and Jeff; the firm could be expanded to shorten waiting times, but that's not in Tom's nature. He prefers to take time to ensure perfection. 'We may not be the fastest,' he says, 'but we are one of the best.'

ESTABLISHED:	1982
LOCATION:	Breinigsville, Pennsylvania, USA
BIKE TYPE MADE:	Titanium and steel frame sets
SPECIALITIES:	Steel, custom hand-built lugs and frames, advanced custom titanium frame engineering
FAVOURITE RIDER:	Marianne Vos
FAVOURITE BICYCLE:	Confenti
FAVOURITE OBJECT:	Sewing-machine treadle

STRONG FRAMES

Citing his junior-high metalwork teacher Mr Earl as a pivotal individual who set him on his way in the bike-building business, Carl Strong quickly lets you know that he's been mad about both bikes and making them his entire life. Whether road racing, commuting on a mountain bike or BMXing with his brother, Carl's early years were filled with cycling memories and achievements – including a mini-bike built from scratch in Mr Earl's class.

It was road racing that enabled Carl to make the leap from buying frames to making them: 'I bought a Columbus tube set and got started. I hand-mitred the tubes, fixtured, aligned and tacked the frame set on a plywood workbench and TIG-welded it,' he says. From then on he was hooked, and began building frames for anyone who could provide him with enough money for materials.

Today, some 3,500 frames later, Carl has become a recognized name in the frame-building fraternity. He builds road, mountain and carbon frames, but his favourite style is cyclocross. He has designed and built his perfect bike, Carl's Personal Blend, a cyclocross dirt/road model available in steel or titanium, with or without fenders, cantilever brakes, long-reach callipers or discs. 'This configuration really is the most versatile type of high-performance bike you can own,' says Carl.

ESTABLISHED:	1993
LOCATION:	Bozeman, Montana, USA
BIKE TYPE MADE:	Custom steel, titanium and carbon-fibre road, cyclocross and mountain bikes
SPECIALITIES:	TIG-welded, lightweight steel road frames
FAVOURITE RIDER:	Tejay van Garderen – 'he worked for us when he was a kid'
FAVOURITE BICYCLE:	Early safety bicycles – 'especially the style with the larger rear wheel and curved tubes'
FAVOURITE OBJECT:	Porsche 917/30

SUPERNOVA DESIGN

Marketing a bicycle on its environmental credentials may seem obvious, but while its steel and composite competitors are quite green, Supernova's Waldmeister model is positively bright green! The frame is made of wood, a renewable material that acts as a CO_2 sink by removing carbon dioxide from the atmosphere. Wood does not become dangerous to the environment during the production process, and it can be thermally processed at the end of its extremely long service life. The frame's optional top layer of rare wood is sustainably harvested, and the water-based glue holding together the thin layers of plywood (up to a hundred of them) is ecologically harmless.

Even the bike's packaging and transport have been thought through. The bike frame is shipped from the producer's workshop near Munich to the assembly plant in Freiburg in reusable wooden boxes. Keeping the production of the frame in southern Germany avoids the usual long-distance transportation of bike frames from producers in low-cost countries. Added to all of these green plus-points is the fact that Supernova's bikes also look cool – a winning formula in today's environmentally conscious, design-loving world.

'The special charm of the Waldmeister lies in the fusion of the natural substances, wood and leather, with high-tech materials like carbon and titanium, and the reduction of everything to the basics,' says its creator Marcus Wallmeyer. 'We strive to make it as environmentally friendly and as beautiful as possible.'

ESTABLISHED:	1997
LOCATION:	Gundelfingen, Germany
BIKE TYPE MADE:	Wood
SPECIALITIES:	No seat tube
FAVOURITE RIDER:	René Wildhaber
FAVOURITE BICYCLE:	'My own, of course!'
FAVOURITE OBJECT:	Supernova Airstream road light

TI CYCLES

Dave Levy, founder of Ti Cycles, has been working as a professional frame-builder since 1986. Having learned the basics of construction technique, geometry design and the science of bicycle fit from the resident frame-builders at R&E Cycles in Seattle, Washington, Dave wanted to build lighter, higher-performance frames in titanium, while continuing to craft custom frames in steel.

He went out on his own in 1990, and since then the company has built over 1,500 frames for clients that range from professionals to novice riders. Ti Cycles relocated from Seattle to Portland, Oregon, in 2002, and commemorated its twentieth anniversary in 2010 with the opening of a new, 214m2 (2,300 sq ft) fabrication facility. Dave has always worked creatively with metals, from building BMX bicycles in high school to metal sculpture at university, where he studied engineering. 'The pride and sensitivity of an artist and craftsman, coupled with the analytical skills of an engineer, are what enable me to create bicycles that are aesthetically appealing and functionally precise,' he says.

As a consequence, Dave isn't afraid to build any type of bike, from mountain and cyclocross to road bikes, and even tandems. 'Whether you ride on or off-road, race or cruise, tour or commute, solo or in tandem, Ti Cycles has the experience to create the perfect bicycle for you,' he says. Dave currently serves as the president of the Oregon Bicycle Constructors Association.

ESTABLISHED:	1990
LOCATION:	Portland, Oregon, USA
BIKE TYPE MADE:	Frames, forks, stems, bars, seat posts, racks and hardware for all types of bike
SPECIALITIES:	'Custom-designed and fabricated bicycles in titanium and steel, which meet riders' needs while fulfilling their cycling dreams'
FAVOURITE RIDER:	Ronnie Schmeer, Andrew Hampsten
FAVOURITE BICYCLE:	Teledyne Titan
FAVOURITE OBJECT:	Acura NSX

TRUE FABRICATION

Road, mountain, cyclocross, track, commuter: Texas-based bicycle-maker True Fabrication builds them all, which is not surprising given that Cody Baron, Clark Davidson and Cole Thompson are three guys who seem to have enjoyed and excelled at almost every cycling discipline out there. Founded in 2005, during a sixteen-hour car journey home from an annual mountain-biking trip to Colorado, the company was the logical next step for the three cycling-mad friends, who had been riding and travelling together for many years.

Over the next year, the trio set about acquiring the necessary tools and mastering their fabrication skills, as well as developing a geometry philosophy, logo and branding, so that they could build first for themselves, and then for others. 'We quickly realized that the bikes we were building [29-in. (74 cm) mountain bikes] were not being built by the major bike manufacturers at that time,' says Cody. 'We started spreading the word about our bikes to our friends in the Austin cycling community, and soon had a small customer base.'

Since then True Fabrication has gone from strength to strength, and the team is always busy in the workshop. But what makes them special? 'We don't build frames to make a living, that's what our day jobs are for,' Cody explains. 'We build frames because we love cycling, and are passionate about frame-building. We don't take short-cuts. Instead, we take the time to ensure that each bike is designed to be perfect for each customer. Each of us can create a custom bicycle from inception to completion, but the combination of our unique talents and abilities makes us a great partnership.'

ESTABLISHED:	2005
LOCATION:	Austin, Texas, USA
BIKE TYPE MADE:	All types of steel bicycles, forks, stems and bicycle racks
SPECIALITIES:	Hardtail 29ers
FAVOURITE RIDER:	[Cole] 'A guy in Ghana, with two goats on his rear rack and another draped around his neck' [Clark] Cobbled-race specialist Andrei Tchmil
FAVOURITE BICYCLE:	[Cole] 'Rick Hunter's bikes, especially the dirt tourer he showed at the 2012 NAHBS' [Clark] 'The first custom road frame I ever bought, built by Brent Steelman'
FAVOURITE OBJECT:	[Cole] The gömböc [Clark] The Gothic arch – 'especially those at York Minster'

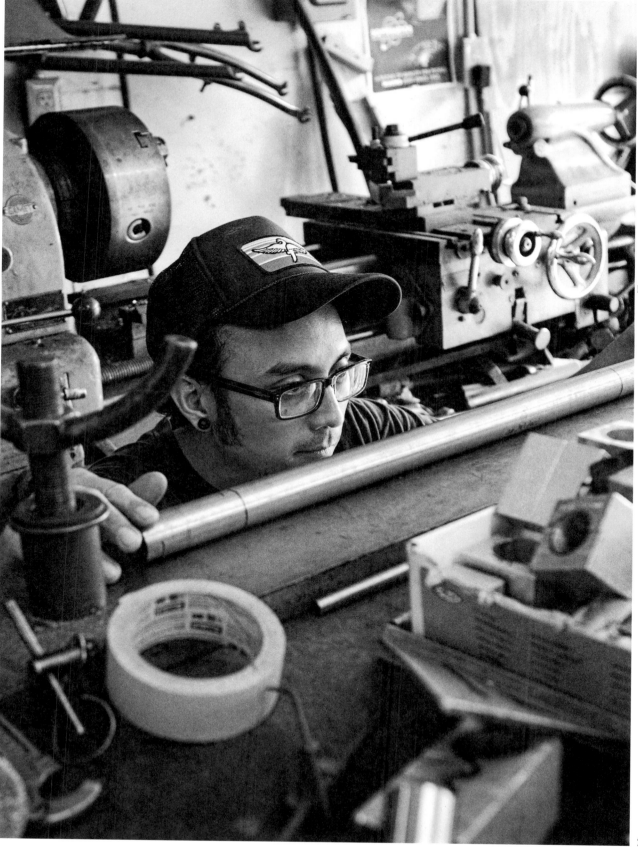

TRUE FABRICATION ∞ USA

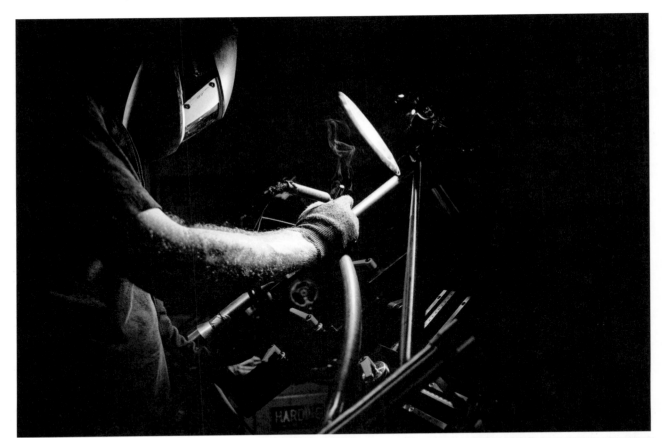

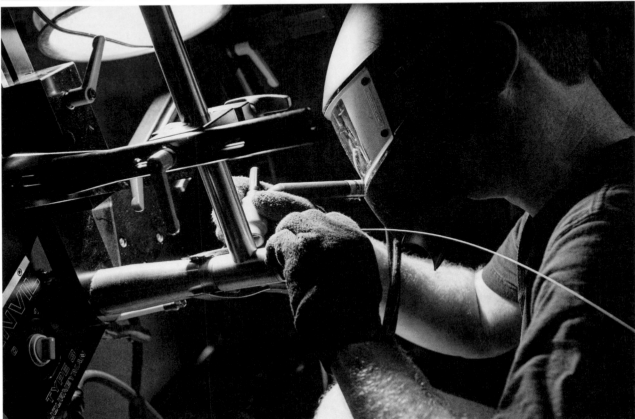

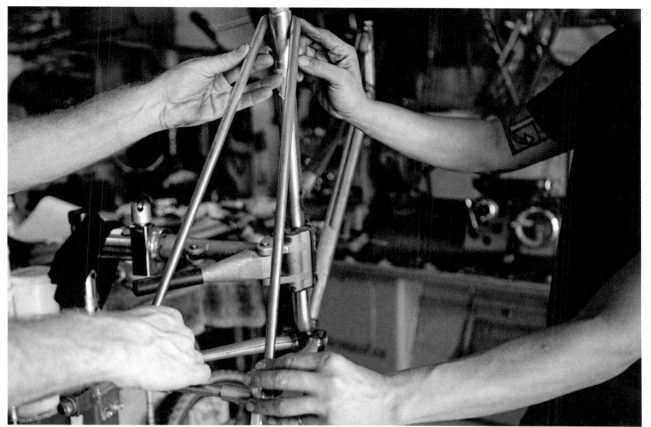

TRUE NORTH CYCLES

True North Cycles was founded in 1993, when Hugh Black began building frames in the workshop of his parents' farm near Alma, in Quebec, Canada. Hugh tells how his dedication to custom frame-building was tested in the early years: 'The workshop was heated by a wood stove, and I had to continually collect firewood to keep warm to work,' he chuckles.

Most of the early frames that Hugh built were mountain bikes, but over time he steadily expanded his repertoire to include frames for other types of cycling. He came to bicycle-making off the back of a degree in mechanical engineering and a desire to not get caught up in the engineering jobs available in the labour market. Fascinated with bicycle manufacturing, Hugh built and rode a number of prototype mountain bikes while at university, and became excited about the possibility of dedicating his own engineering skills and attention to detail to bicycle frame-building full time.

Today, the company is based in Belwood, Ontario. It has a fully heated workshop, and produces around a hundred frames a year. These can be anything from mountain bikes (Hugh's first love) to touring, cyclocross or road bikes. 'I like to think that I have managed to merge my passions for bicycles, engineering and craftsmanship,' he says. 'And the result is True North Cycles.'

ESTABLISHED:	1993
LOCATION:	Belwood, Ontario, Canada
SPECIALITIES:	Custom steel and titanium road, cyclocross, touring, tandem, commuter and mountain bikes
FAVOURITE BICYCLE:	'My ten-year-old single-speed cyclocross/commuter bike'
FAVOURITE OBJECT:	'Anything bicycle-design related'

TSUKUMO CYCLE SPORTS

Tsukumo Cycle Sports, world-famous for its Kalavinka brand, is the company showcasing the brilliance of master frame-builder Aiko Tanabe. Having been a cyclist since he was a boy, Aiko graduated to competing in amateur Keirin races, where he caught the eye of Hiroyasu Shimizu of Kofu Bicycles. Shimizu, recognizing his talent, recruited him as a test rider for new products.

'I was part of the Hosei University cycling team for four years, before moving to the Maruishi bicycle team and training for the 1972 Summer Olympics,' Aiko says. Despite failing to make the Olympics team, he was selected two years later to ride in the World Championships in Montreal. Finding that his fellow riders wanted better-made frames, he decided to learn frame-building from Toshio Kajiwara, the maker of the frames he had been racing. 'I learned a lot about frame-making from Kajiwara,' says Aiko. 'I was always thinking about ways to optimize the balance of the bike for the rider. Furthermore, I'm now always careful not to overstress the materials used to construct the frame.'

Since then, Aiko's frames have been sought after by a global clientele. They are still used in Keirin racing, a phenomenon that has fuelled interest in custom-built bikes in Japan. Recently, demand has increased as Europe and America have caught on to the sport and the exquisitely simple designs produced by its frame-builders. 'Because of Keirin, Japan never really had the decline in custom-built bikes that other countries, such as Italy, did,' says Aiko. 'I think the resurgence of interest today is good. A new generation of people are becoming aware of custom-built bikes.'

ESTABLISHED:	1975
LOCATION:	Tokyo, Japan
BIKE TYPE MADE:	Road, track
SPECIALITIES:	Keirin frames – 'from a rider's point of view'
FAVOURITE RIDER:	Eddy Merckx, Daniel Morelon
FAVOURITE BICYCLE:	Toshio Kajiwara frames
FAVOURITE OBJECT:	'I like smooth and minimal designs'

TSUNEHIRO CYCLES

Tsunehiro Cycles is based in cycling Mecca: Portland, Oregon. The company was launched in 2008, just one year after engineering, welding and frame-building graduate (that's three different courses, before budding frame-builders get excited) Rob Tsunehiro began building bicycle frames. His business partner is industrial designer Silas Beebe, also based in Oregon, who has tackled such diverse products as snowboarding boots, bathroom taps and barbeques. The two joined forces for the Oregon Manifest cargo bike-building competition, and the result was an all-reflective cargo bike that took second place.

'My inspiration for the bike's design was seeing people trying to carry a variety of cargo and passengers,' says Silas. 'That, and the dull, utilitarian styling and unnecessary extra weight of existing cargo bikes. What I wanted to do was design and build the ultimate urban utility bike, thus amplifying helpful innovations in day-to-day practicality and safety with style.'

While Silas's strength lies in design, Rob had the necessary bike-building skills, and the two made a formidable team in the competition, which saw tricycles, recumbents and cable-steered bikes entering the fray. Their design is powder-coated to make the entire frame reflective at night, and has a removable seat for passengers, an integrated tube lock, a phone charger and even a 360°-visibility, handlebar-stem spacer ring light.

ESTABLISHED:	2008
LOCATION:	Portland, Oregon, USA
BIKE TYPE MADE:	Endurance road, gravel grinder, touring, commuting
SPECIALITIES:	Technologically advanced steel bicycles
FAVOURITE RIDER:	'Our friend Michael Sylvester, who won the Laurelwood Road Hillclimb back in the day – possibly not his grandest racing achievement, but we really like the climb'
FAVOURITE BICYCLE:	'Sacha White's Vanilla bikes consistently push that bar'

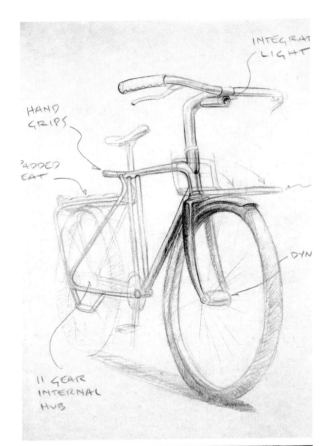

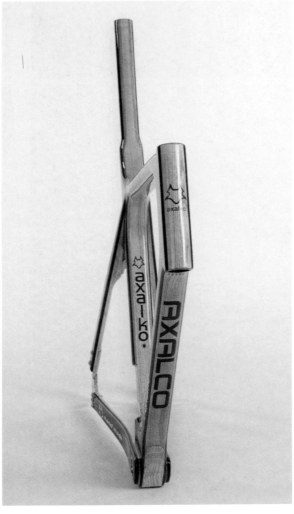

TXIRBIL KOOPERATIVA ELKARTEA

Carpenters who make bicycles are unusual. Carpenters who design and make high-tech bikes to showcase their expertise in thermal-wood modification are even more unusual, but that's what Enrique Ardura and brothers Aitzol and Andoitz Tellería do in their workshop in Bilbao, Spain. The result is BAT, a high-performance racing bike, built from laminated pieces of wood that together create a frame of amazing strength and perfect elasticity. 'We spent two years developing a frame that makes the most of wood's inherent strength,' explains Enrique. 'It combines an ash core with a micro-laminated finish that optimizes its rigidity and resistance.'

Lignin and cellulose, both found in wood, provide a magnificent weight–strength ratio – a fact fully exploited by the team. Lignin causes the cell walls to become rigid with a compressive strength of 2,400 kg/cm2 (that's higher than concrete), while the cellulose fibres held together by the lignin binder have a tensile strength of 10,000 kg/cm2, which superior to steel. After fully researching the potential of their idea, the team came to the conclusion that wood's tubular fibres were perfect for creating a fast, sturdy bicycle frame. They also understood that in addition to looking great, wood is resistant and can absorb a high level of vibration and be manufactured in small but strong sections – much lighter than generally perceived.

With this common but super-strong raw material, the team design and manufacture handmade ash-cored frames that are customized to each client's size and colour preferences. 'We're fans of bikes and mountain sports, and together we were inspired to develop a bike that combined our knowledge of the inherent properties and potential of wood with our leisure-time activities,' says Enrique. 'We're very pleased with the result!'

ESTABLISHED:	2006
LOCATION:	Bilbao, Spain
BIKE TYPE MADE:	Road
SPECIALITIES:	Wooden frames
FAVOURITE RIDER:	Gorka Izagirre
FAVOURITE BICYCLE:	Brompton
FAVOURITE OBJECT:	The wooden chassis of a Morgan car

VAN HULSTEIJN BICYCLES

The Van Hulsteijn blog is almost as cryptic as the design of the company's handmade frames: 'I guess I looked frightened when I first saw Charlie,' begins one post. 'With his mask and all. With his pneumatic arms. With his go-go gadget legs. With his blowtorch. With his metallic laughter that can be heard blocks away and keeps little children out of their sleep.'

But scary or not, Charlie is the backbone of a bicycle-maker of incredible individuality. Charlie is the welder, described as 'what the monster was for Dr Frankenstein. What the beast was for the beauty.' He crafts wonderfully unusual frames from stainless steel in five different sizes; after that, the choice of frame colour, rim material (wood rims are available) and accessories are down to the client. The firm takes just two to four weeks to complete a bicycle, after an initial consultation regarding dimensions and colour preferences.

Van Hulsteijn bikes are growing in popularity, and are now shipped around the world. The company is also starting to offer frames and other parts separately, now that Frank (their IT guy) has warmed to Charlie. 'Everybody is scared of Charlie in the beginning,' continues the blog. 'Everybody loves him in the end. So does Frank. It is said that Frank sometimes even hugs Charlie. In return, Charlie lights his cigarette with his blowtorch. Without Charlie, we wouldn't be here selling bicycles.'

ESTABLISHED:	2008
LOCATION:	Arnhem, Netherlands
BIKE TYPE MADE:	City bikes
SPECIALITIES:	Bikes that are fully handmade from stainless steel
FAVOURITE RIDER:	Erik Damhuis
FAVOURITE BICYCLE:	Francesco Moser's bike designs

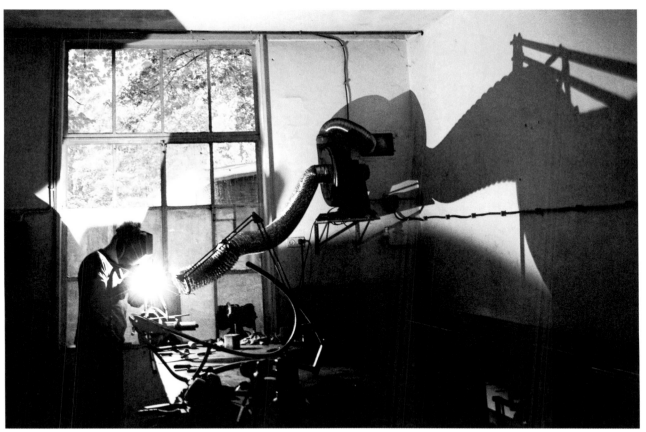

WINTER BICYCLES

Based in Springfield, Oregon, Winter Bicycles is the marque of Eric Estlund, who bills himself as a 'designer, builder, email guy and official floor sweeper'. Eric has always had an affinity with bicycles. In his college years, he worked as a bicycle advocate to help bring more people and bikes together. 'I've led both road and off-road tours for children and adults,' he says, 'and continue to work as an advocate and teacher to promote safe, community-minded sport and commuter cycling.'

Today, Eric utilizes the knowledge garnered from his art degree – for which he focused on metal sculpture – to build bicycles for a varied client base. 'I can work with you to help design your perfect daily-driver city bike, your health-conscious trainer or your event-specific competition machine,' he says. The bicycles are made from a custom blend of steel tubing to be purpose-built and rider-centric. 'That means that each frame, each detail, is designed to fit your needs and desires for your riding style, tastes and environment,' Eric explains, 'whether it's a rainy-day commuter, a Sunday cruiser or a thoroughbred racer.'

And the name? Winter is generally considered the off-season for competitive cyclists, but, as many cyclists know, it is a great time for both long training rides and casual group rides. 'Winter is cycling's best-kept secret,' Eric says. 'My goal is to build bikes with this sense of year-round versatility combined with fresh, clean design. I want to build you a bike you are excited to ride every day of the year.'

ESTABLISHED:	2008
LOCATION:	Springfield, Oregon, USA
BIKE TYPE MADE:	Individually tailored frames, forks, racks and stems
SPECIALITIES:	Road and track bikes; high-performance non-racing bikes
FAVOURITE BICYCLE:	'One built with love and precision, and ridden as intended'

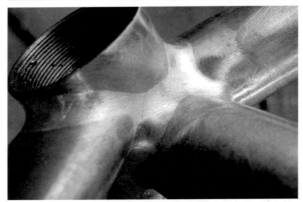

WREN BICYCLES

Founded in 2010, Wren Bicycles produces around five hundred bikes per year. The Wren Original, a three-speed, city-cycling model equipped with bespoke luggage racks, combines the charm of a vintage bicycle with the practicality of contemporary design and components. Its compact frame is especially suited to cyclists who find traditional town bicycles too cumbersome.

Founder Peter Richardson came up with the design after his girlfriend found it difficult to find a bike design to suit her needs. 'She wanted something that was compact and manageable without feeling flimsy,' he recalls, 'but traditional upright bikes proved to be too large and unwieldy, while the ride quality and practicality of most folding bikes were unconvincing.' Being a keen cyclist and bicycle restorer, Peter already had a good understanding of the ins and outs of parts and fittings. He started off with sketches, incorporating the features he felt would be most useful, and things developed from there. Wren's first bicycle was made available to the public in 2011. Peter now designs bikes for clients, with the designs manufactured by another company. His girlfriend's influence, as well as that of the American handmade scene, has turned him into a champion of British hand-built bicycles.

'Hopefully we will see a continued resurgence in smaller hand-built makers, especially in the UK,' he says. 'It would be great if we could reintroduce larger-scale manufacturing back to Britain, too, though this will likely only happen once all the cheap labour opportunities in the developing world have been fully exploited.'

ESTABLISHED:	2010
LOCATION:	London, UK
BIKE TYPE MADE:	City, commuter
SPECIALITIES:	Small wheels, utility, practicality
FAVOURITE RIDER:	Miguel Indurain or Mr Hoopdriver
FAVOURITE BICYCLE:	Achielle Sam Deluxe 3-speed
FAVOURITE OBJECT:	Blackwell House, Cumbria

YIPSAN

Renold Yip is Cantonese, but he was born and raised in Hong Kong, and grew up immersed in the cultural mix of East and West that permeates the city. When still relatively young, Renold went to the UK to study, where he received a degree in engineering. Next stop, in 2002, was the US, where he began working in bike shops. As with many a story like Renold's, bike-building was the logical progression, and he became certified as a fit specialist. Today, he designs and builds award-winning bikes from his studio in Fort Collins, Colorado, specializing in steel, with a repertoire that includes road, cyclocross, track, randonneuring and off-road bicycles.

But this impressive list doesn't convey the depth of engineering and two-wheeled travel history in Renold's family. His first name may give a clue, however: 'My father named me Renold for a very important reason,' he says. 'He was a long-time motorcycle enthusiast, especially of Triumph, Norton and BSA. During that era, a famous motorcycle chain was made by Renold (they made bicycle chains, too). My dad believed that a motorcycle chain is small in size, but very efficient and important to the operation of a motorbike. There you have it! I was named after a motorbike chain.'

Renold laughs as he says, 'If I follow this custom, I may have to name my child Shimano, Sram or Wippermann!'

ESTABLISHED:	2007
LOCATION:	Fort Collins, Colorado, USA
BIKE TYPE MADE:	Steel road, randonneur, touring and mountain bikes
SPECIALITIES:	Traditional bicycles, made with hand tools
FAVOURITE BICYCLE:	Moulton
FAVOURITE OBJECT:	Alfa Romeo cars

ZINN CYCLES

When you're six-and-a-half feet tall, getting the right bike is not a simple matter of picking up a factory frame from the local dealer. And when you're racing for the US national team, you really want a bike that fits properly. The trouble is, sponsors don't always make them.

This is what Lennard Zinn discovered when racing for the USA, and his predicament spurred him on to found a company that builds bikes specifically for tall people – and shorter ones, too, if they ask nicely. 'My height meant that I required custom frames to fit me properly,' says Lennard, 'and the fact that tall frames tend to shimmy provided me with the impetus to solve both of those problems. I built my first frame by following the instructions in *The Proteus Framebuilding Handbook*, and then I really learned the trade while working for Tom Ritchey, building fillet-brazed steel mountain bikes.'

Lennard's degree in Physics from Colorado College gave him the knowledge and requisite skills to solve the problem of the high-speed shimmy, and his senior seminar focused on bike stability (he even wrote a computer model for calculating it). Since founding Zinn Cycles in 1982, Lennard has built around fifty to sixty-five custom bikes each year. He is constantly innovating, and in 2008 the company began making custom integrated-spindle cranks.

ESTABLISHED:	1982
LOCATION:	Boulder, Colorado, USA
BIKE TYPE MADE:	Custom road, coupled travel, hardtail mountain, cyclocross, tandem and track bikes in titanium, magnesium or steel; full-suspension mountain bikes in aluminium
SPECIALITIES:	Bikes for big and tall people
FAVOURITE RIDER:	Taylor Phinney
FAVOURITE BICYCLE:	Volagi – 'for the innovation to come up with something new and the courage to fight for its principles'
FAVOURITE OBJECT:	Neuschwanstein Castle, Bavaria

ZULLO BIKE

Tiziano Zullo was born in 1952, in Stallavena, a small village near Verona in the north of Italy. Like many of his peers, he cycled everywhere as a child, touring the hilly countryside around his home. At the age of fourteen, he began racing – road races in the summer, cyclocross in winter – entering both local and national events. Soon another, if related, love came into his life: 'In the early 1970s, I came into contact with the world of frame-building through the Italian artisans, who were renowned for their skills,' Tiziano says. 'Soon I, too, was building frames. That was the start of a very steep learning curve.'

He established his company in 1973, and became a recognized frame-builder, exporting his brand to Germany, France, Australia and the USA. In 1985, Tiziano met with top Dutch professional team TVM, and was their frame supplier from 1986 to 1992, building bicycles for such well-known racers as Phil Anderson, Dimitri Konyshev, Jesper Skibby and Scott Sunderland. Today, Tiziano is still involved in the production of some frames, mainly those made in steel, as well as remaining responsible for all of the frame graphics and some of the frame painting.

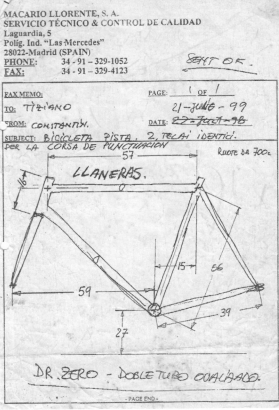

ESTABLISHED:	1973
LOCATION:	Castelnuovo del Garda, Italy
BIKE TYPE MADE:	Road frames, track, cyclocross, time trial
SPECIALITIES:	Inqubo, a super-stiff frame made in collaboration with Dedacciai
FAVOURITE RIDER:	Phil Anderson

DIRECTORY

ACHIELLE
Brugsesteenweg 203,
8740 Egem (Pittem), Belgium
achielle.be

ANDERSON CYCLES
P.O. Box 280332,
St Paul, Minnesota 55128, USA
andersoncustombicycles.com

ART & INDUSTRY
Portland, Oregon, USA
artandindustry.wordpress.com

ATELIERS D'EMBELLIE
Grenoble, France
ateliersembellie.com

A-TRAIN CYCLES
2718 E. 27th Street,
Minneapolis,
Minnesota 55406, USA
atraincycles.com

BAUM CYCLES
7 Seabright Street,
North Shore, Victoria 3214,
Australia
baumcycles.com

BELOVED CYCLES
Portland, Oregon, USA
belovedcycles.com

BIKE BY ME
Saltmätargatan 22,
11 359 Stockholm, Sweden
bikebyme.com

BISHOP BIKES
Baltimore, Maryland, USA
bishopbikes.com

BOHEMIAN BICYCLES
5618 E. Linden Street,
Tucson, Arizona 85712, USA
bohemianbicycles.com

BONDI BEACH CRUISERS
68 Blair Street, North Bondi,
New South Wales 2026,
Australia
bondibeachcruisers.com.au

BUSYMAN BICYCLES
Melbourne, Victoria, Australia
busymanbicycles.blogspot.co.uk

GARRETT CHOW
15130 Concord Circle,
Morgan Hill, California 95037,
USA
specialized.com

CICLI MAESTRO
Milan, Italy
ciclimaestromilano.com

CIELO CYCLES
2801 NW Nela Street,
Portland, Oregon 97210, USA
cielo.chrisking.com

CIRCLE A CYCLES
523 Charles Street,
Providence,
Rhode Island 02904, USA
circleacycles.com

COAST CYCLES
50 Troutman Street,
Brooklyn, New York 11206, USA
johnnycoast.com

COLUMBINE CYCLE WORKS
10740 Calypso Lane,
Mendocino, California 95460,
USA
columbinecycle.com

CONCEPT BIKES
Burnaby, British Columbia,
Canada
concept-bikes.com

CORIMA
ZA de Champgrand,
Sortie Autoroute A7,
26270 Loriol-sur-Drôme, France
corima.com

DESALVO CUSTOM CYCLES
255 Helman Street, Suite 3A,
Ashland, Oregon 97520, USA
desalvocycles.com

DETROIT BICYCLE COMPANY
Detroit, Michigan, USA
detroitbicyclecompany.com

TORKEL DOHMERS
Stockholm, Sweden
redtop.se

DONHOU BICYCLES
Hackney, London, UK
donhoubicycles.com

ELLIS CYCLES
500 Racine Street,
Waterford, Wisconsin 53185,
USA
elliscycles.com

ENGIN CYCLES
7837 Germantown Avenue,
Philadelphia,
Pennsylvania 19118, USA
engincycles.com

ENIGMA BIKES
13 Apex Park,
Diplocks Way, Hailsham,
East Sussex BN27 3JU, UK
enigmabikes.com

EYE TO HAND
London, UK
eyetohand.com

FARADAY BICYCLES
San Francisco, California, USA
faradaybikes.com

ALEX FERNÁNDEZ CAMPS
Barcelona, Spain
alexfernandezcamps.com

FIREFLY BICYCLES
117 Boston Street,
Boston, Massachusetts 02125,
USA
fireflybicycles.com

FOFFA BIKES
9 Pinchin Street,
London E1 1SA, UK
foffabikes.com

FRANCES CYCLES
203 Cedar Street,
Santa Cruz, California 95060,
USA
francescycles.com

GEEKHOUSE BIKES
12 Channel Street, #202,
Boston, Massachusetts 02210,
USA
geekhousebikes.com ·

BRUCE GORDON CYCLES
409 Petaluma Boulevard S,
Petaluma, California 94952, USA
bgcycles.com

GREENSPEED
Unit 5/31 Rushdale Street,
Knoxfield, Victoria 3180,
Australia
greenspeed.com.au

HILLBRICK BICYCLES
Unit 12, 141 Hartley Road,
Smeaton Grange,
New South Wales 2567,
Australia
hillbrick.com.au

JOSÉ HURTADO
Madrid, Spain
josehurtado.eu

ICARUS FRAMES
Austin, Texas, USA
icarusframes.com

JAEGHER
Bruggestraat 120,
8755 Ruiselede, Belgium
jaegher.com

JEFF JONES BICYCLES
8000 Griffin Creek Road,
Medford, Oregon 97501, USA
jonesbikes.com

KINFOLK BICYCLE CO
90 Wythe Avenue,
Brooklyn, New York 11211, USA
Kamimeguro, Meguro,
Tokyo 153-0051, Japan
kinfolklife.com

KONNO CYCLE WORKS
Tokyo, Japan
cherubim.jp

CHRIS KVALE CYCLES
2637 27th Avenue S.,
Minneapolis, Minnesota 55406,
USA
chriskvalecycles.com

LENZ SPORT
Denver, Colorado, USA
lenzsport.com

LLEWELLYN CUSTOM BICYCLES
Brisbane, Queensland 4000
Australia
llewellynbikes.com

MING CYCLE INDUSTRIAL CO
No. 50, Ln. 462,
Guangxing Road, Taiping
District, Taichung 411, Taiwan
mingcycle.com.tw

MISSION BICYCLE COMPANY
766 Valencia Street,
San Francisco, California 94110,
USA
missionbicycle.com

MOULTON BICYCLE COMPANY
Holt Road, Bradford on Avon,
Wiltshire BA15 1AH, UK
moultonbicycles.co.uk

NAKED
1039 Gowlland Harbour Road,
Quadra Island, British Columbia,
Canada
timetogetnaked.com

NAZCA LIGFIETSEN
Dorpsstraat 67,
7948 BM Nijeveen, Netherlands
nazca-ligfietsen.nl

MARC NEWSON
7 Howick Place,
London SW1P 1BB, UK
marc-newson.com

NOBILETTE CYCLES
2563 Horseshoe Circle W,
Longmont, Colorado 80504,
USA

NORWID
Bauerweg 40,
25335 Neuendorf bei Elmshorn,
Germany
norwid.de

MIKULÁŠ NOVOTNÝ
Prague, Czech Republic
mikulasnovotny.tumblr.com

PAULUS QUIROS
Unit 1.15, Dyfatty Park,
Burry Port, Carmarthenshire
SA16 0FB, UK
paulusquiros.co.uk

PEGORETTI CICLI
Via dei Golden 3,
38052 Caldonazzo, Italy
pegoretticicli.com

PETOV DESIGN
Gelnica, Slovakia
petovdesign.com

PONY BIKES
87 Capel St West, Melbourne,
Victoria 3003, Australia
ponybikes.com

PRIMATE FRAMES
17 Chalmers Street, Balgownie,
New South Wales 2519, Australia
primateframes.com.au

NEIL PRYDE BIKES
20/F YKK Building,
Phase 2, No 2 San Lik Street,
Tuen Mun, Hong Kong 00000,
China
neilprydebikes.com

RETROVELO
Lützner Straße 75,
04177 Leipzig, Germany
retrovelo.de

ROCK LOBSTER CYCLES
2533-D Mission Street Ext.,
Santa Cruz, California 95060,
USA
rocklobstercycles.com

ROUNDTAIL
Windsor, Ontario, Canada
roundtail.ca

RUNOUT INDUSTRIES
Canmore, Alberta, Canada
runout-industries.com

SAFFRON FRAMEWORKS
254–255 Grosvenor Terrace,
Camberwell, London SE5 0NP,
UK
saffronframeworks.com

SANITOV
Denmark
sanitov.com

SANOMAGIC
Shinkiba 1–6–12, Koutouku,
Tokyo 136-0082, Japan
sanomagic.world.coocan.jp

SCHINDELHAUER BIKES
Schlesische Straße 27,
10997 Berlin, Germany
schindelhauerbikes.com

SHAND CYCLES
3B Nasmyth Court,
Houston Industrial Estate,
Livingston,
West Lothian EH54 5EG, UK
shandcycles.com

SIGNAL CYCLES
60 N. Page Street,
Portland, Oregon 97227, USA
signalcycles.com

SIX-ELEVEN BICYCLE CO
Roanoke, Virginia, USA
sixelevenbicycleco.com

SMAN CRUISERS
Hoorn, Netherlands
smancruisers.com

SPECTRUM CYCLES
1190 Dorney Road,
Breinigsville,
Pennsylvania 18031, USA
spectrum-cycles.com

STRONG FRAMES
619 S. Willson Avenue,
Bozeman, Montana 59715, USA
strongframes.com

SUPERNOVA DESIGN
Industriestraße 26,
79194 Gundelfingen, Germany
supernova-design.com

TI CYCLES
15707 N.W. McNamee Road,
Portland, Oregon 97231, USA
ticycles.com

TRUE FABRICATION
Austin, Texas, USA
truefabricationbicycles.com

TRUE NORTH CYCLES
Belwood, Ontario, Canada
truenorthcycles.com

TSUKUMO CYCLE SPORTS
1–16–21 Meguro-Honcho,
Meguro-ku, Tokyo 152-0002,
Japan
kalavinka-bikes.com

TSUNEHIRO CYCLES
4629 SE 17th Avenue,
Portland, Oregon 97202, USA
tsunehirocycles.com

TXIRBIL KOOPERATIVA ELKARTEA
Bilbao, Spain

VAN HULSTEIJN BICYCLES
Klarendalseweg 372,
6822 Arnhem, Netherlands
vanhulsteijn.com

WINTER BICYCLES
Springfield, Oregon, USA
winterbicycles.com

WREN BICYCLES
Unit 4, 49–59 Old Street,
London EC1V 9HX, UK
wrenbicycles.co.uk

YIPSAN
Fort Collins, Colorado, USA
yipsanbicycles.com

ZINN CYCLES
7437 S. Boulder Road,
Boulder, Colorado 80303, USA
zinncycles.com

ZULLO BIKE
Via Sei Fontane, 10,
37014 Castelnuovo del Garda,
Italy
zullo-bike.com

INDEX

I would like to thank all the bicycle makers included within this book for their willingness to provide images and information, and for their patience in dealing with an author relatively new to the cycling world. Many thanks are also due to the design and production team involved with this book, and to everyone at Thames & Hudson. You have all been instrumental in creating this wonderful publication.

PHOTO CREDITS

Ginko Photo (ginko-photo.com) 11, 78–9; Florian Gill 12, 222–7; Vincent Dominguez 16–17; 150–5; Eva Vlonck 18–21; Eden Mac 30–3; Ellie Kingsley 34–5; Chris Milliman 40 (top); Todd Gardner 40 (bottom), 41; Joshua Oldfield Photography 52–3; Feride Peel 54–7; Cicli Maestro 62–3; Dylan VanWeelden/Chris King Precision Components 64–7; Milt Borchert 74 (bottom); John Murphy 74–5; Brian McDivitt 75 (top left); Tim Tidball Photography 80–1, 140–3; Tristan Conor Holden, Andi Sapey, Hal Shinnie 88–91; Drew Triplett, Peter DiAntoni 92–3; Charles Uniatowski Photography 94–7; Faraday Bicycles 104–7; Tyson Sadlo 114–17; Jan Sidgwick 136–9; Will Goodan 144–5; Nick Wigston 156–7, 278–9; Robert Cobcroft (veloaficionado.com), Mary Ann Martin 158–9; Kristin Fox 164–7; Naked 170–1; Henk van der Woerdt 172–3; Marc Newson Ltd 174–5; Mark Nobilette 176–7; Norwid (norwid.de) 178–9; Kayti Peschke 183; Gunter Binsack 202; Tortola International, Inc. 206, 207 (bottom); Antoni Kupnicki 207 (top); Chris Read 208–9; Jeremy Fokkens 210–11; Casper Helmer 214–17; Jim Johnstone 228 (top and middle); Russell Stout 228 (bottom), 229 (top); David Hungate 232–5; Stefan Warnar 236–9; Loretta Strong 242–5; Christian Rokosch 246–9; Eric J. Herboth 250–1; Sarah M. Bremer 252–7; Tsukumo Cycle Sports 260–1; Winter Bicycles 270–1

To my wife Stephanie, who puts up with my incessant moaning when things just don't go right.

First published in the United Kingdom in 2014 by Thames & Hudson Ltd, 181A High Holborn, London WC1V 7QX

The Bicycle Artisans © 2014 Will Jones

Designed by Barnbrook

British Library Cataloguing-in-Publication Data

A catalogue record for this book is available from the British Library

ISBN 978-0-500-51729-1

Manufactured in Singapore by Imago

To find out about all our publications, please visit **www.thamesandhudson.com**. There you can subscribe to our e-newsletter, browse or download our current catalogue, and buy any titles that are in print.